1

CW00381654

Contents

Sarum Chronicle is published on behalf of its editorial team by Hobnob Press, P O Box 1838, East Knoyle, Salisbury SP3 6FA, to whom all orders, correspondence and contributions for future issues should be addressed. Potential contributors are invited to apply for a style sheet.

Front cover illustration: Dinton Church from the south. See pp. 37-49. (photograph by John Chandler)

Introduction

L
ike its predecessors this fourth annual issue of *Sarum Chronicle* contains a varied selection of historical research from the Salisbury area. John Chandler uses old maps and documents to suggest the possible location of the medieval borough of Old Sarum, and shows how this planted settlement may be traced in the present-day topography of Stratford-sub-Castle. Sue Johnson has researched some of the problems faced by the Fisherton Anger Burial Board in the creation of Devizes Road Cemetery. She also contributes information about Miss Child to a short paper by Steve Hobbs, who examines evidence to support the authenticity of an account of the 1627 plague which Miss Child preserved. To coincide with its 150th anniversary Peter Blacklock tells of Salisbury's links with the Charge of the Light Brigade in 1854, and Tim Tatton-Brown provides a fascinating insight into the construction of the Cathedral Treasury and Muniment Room, which formerly housed the Magna Carta. Salisbury architect, Michael Drury considers the influence of the Victorian architect, William Butterfield in the Salisbury area, particularly in his restoration work at St Mary's Church, Dinton. Richard Durman identifies how mathematical tiles were used in eighteenth-century Salisbury to modernize buildings, and the locations where they may be seen in the city. We are pleased to include also a short contribution about the Avon Navigation by Michael Cowan (who as chairman of the Hatcher Review Trust helped us to establish *Sarum Chronicle*), in response to a paper we published last year.

Contributions to future issues of *Sarum Chronicle* are always appreciated – articles, short notes and comments, book reviews. We would also value your comments and feedback. Brief guidelines are available for those wishing to write articles and may be obtained from one of the editorial team or via Hobnob Press.

Sarum Chronicle was established in 2001 following the cessation of the *Hatcher Review*, to publish annually historical articles about Salisbury and its district. The editorial team consists (in alphabetical order) of John Chandler, John Elliott, Jane Howells, Sue Johnson, Ruth Newman and Margaret Smith. It is published on behalf of the team by Hobnob Press. To try to ensure its continued success, we have established a subscription list (with the option of payment by standing order or invoice). Membership of the list will guarantee your copy of each newly published issue at the special discounted price for subscribers. Please indicate your interest by completing the enclosed form and returning it promptly to Hobnob Press.

Fisherton Anger (Salisbury Devizes Road) Cemetery 1856-1904

Sue Johnson

After what the *Salisbury Journal* described in its account[1] of the consecration ceremony as the 'many difficulties' encountered by the Burial Board in the creation of the cemetery its members must have hoped for an easier time once it had officially opened on 1 May 1856. However by the end of the first 12 months they had already faced a variety of problems including vandalism, dead plants, the difficulties of locating grave spaces and a request for a lodge at the cemetery.

The lack of provision for an on-site caretaker in the original plans seems to be a serious oversight, especially since the cemetery was so far from the town, though perhaps it was made to keep costs down. When the cemetery had only been open a few months there appears to have been a move to build a lodge, as among the surviving papers is a formal request to the Clerk for a special meeting on 18 February 1857 to consider the matter. Curiously there is no record of a meeting on that date, nor any mention of the subject in the minutes of either the Burial Board or Fisherton Anger Vestry. As time passed and the number of burials increased so did the need for someone to be resident on the site.

In April 1864 the Board directed John Harding of Salisbury, the architect who acted as its Surveyor, to prepare a design which would 'harmonize with the Cemetery Chapels'. Having approved the plans he produced they requested a vestry meeting to authorise borrowing the sum required (£350) and proceeding with the building. However, the churchwardens refused to call a meeting for that purpose and no further progress was made for over a year. Finally in July 1865 the necessary approval was granted – but only for the expenditure of £250. Mr Harding amended his plans to bring down the costs of constructing the lodge and its well to within the sum authorised and tenders for the work were invited. It was February the following year before the contracts with Mr Edward Simper, who loaned the money, and Messrs Harris & Brown, builders of Fisherton, were drawn up. The existing entrance to the cemetery – tower, privy, gate piers and one bay of wall – were demolished to make way for the lodge, with material from them being re-used wherever possible.[2]

- EAST - ELEVATION -

- GROUND - PLAN -

The Lodge. The architect specified cavity walls, an early reference to this type of construction

Six months later with the lodge almost finished the Board turned their attention to who should occupy it. Wanting the same person to act as both sexton and lodgekeeper they first offered the post to William Lucas, the existing sexton. He declined, (but continued to act as sexton) and the job was advertised.[3] The successful applicant was George Scammell who started work in October 1866. His principal duties were keeping the chapels clean and tidy, gardening at both the cemetery and the old churchyard, and constant attendance on the entrance gates either in person or providing a substitute.

The 1871 Census[4] reveals George (age 62) with his wife Maria (56), grand-daughter Rosa (19) and boarder George Trigle (20) in residence. By the standards of the time the lodge with its three bedrooms was a comfortable home with various 'mod cons'. The washhouse had a galvanised iron boiler for heating water plus a Tisbury stone sink and there was a well near at hand to supply water. The building also contained the Waiting Room (or Board Room) which had been furnished by Arthur Foley of the Machine Cabinet Works, Fisherton Street (a Board member) with window blinds, matting, six gothic chairs and a table. This had a no doubt impressive enamelled slate chimney piece (cost 50 shillings) while the living room had to make do with one made, like the sink, from Tisbury stone.

George Scammell remained as lodgekeeper until 1875 when he tendered his resignation with effect from 29 September due to age and ill health. His successor was Edwin Rose, son of George Rose a local man, and a former policeman. His impressive set of testimonials (references) is preserved among the cemetery papers and includes letters from several influential Fisherton citizens and two Chief Constables. The Rose family must have been far more cramped in the lodge than their predecessors. By census night on 3 April 1881[5] there were eight of them – Edwin (38) his wife Mary (44) and their six children aged between 14 and eight months. This was perhaps the reason for the first of two major episodes of building work during their tenure.

In 1878 enlargements and alterations to provide another room were carried out by Abel Harris, to plans prepared by Fred Bath, architect, both local men. The work, costing £80 10s 0d, was to be completed by February 1879, with a penalty clause of £3 per week, though allowance was to be made for delays due to inclement weather. For reasons which are unspecified the work remained unfinished by July and eventually Mr Bath was authorised to complete the extension and deduct the cost from the amount still owed to Mr Harris.

The vestry's refusal to grant the sum first asked for to build the lodge necessitated certain design changes, including a tiled roof instead of slates. This seems to have been ultimately responsible for the second bout of building work the Rose family endured. In March 1891 the lodgekeeper had reported that during a heavy snowstorm so much had drifted under the roof that he had to seek help and eventually removed two cartloads of it. In November 1892 the architect, having inspected the roof thoroughly, declared that it was covered with local tiles, laid with only a shallow lap, many of them decayed and on the whole 'more or less porous'. The gutters did not project far enough so the ends of the roof timbers had rotted, and the ceilings needed to be replaced. The consecrated chapel also needed to be re-roofed and the following year the contractor, Gilbert Harris of Fisherton, started work on both buildings. All together the repairs cost £117 4s 0d, almost half the original cost of the building the lodge.

The water supply for the lodge came from its own well. At first a bucket and windlass were used to obtain water but in 1882 tenders were received for a pump. That of G Edgar of Bedwin Street, Salisbury, survives and reveals that the well was 155 feet deep. He did not get the job – E Tryhorn carried out the work, although perhaps his standards were not high enough as in February 1884 the lodgekeeper complained that he could not get water. Messrs Carters carried out some work which seemed to cure the problem for a time, though they were called out again two years later. In August 1887 there were further problems and the Board directed Mr Brittan (nurseryman) to deliver water to the lodge twice a day until it could be obtained again from the well. There are no further references to absence of water but in 1894 the lodgekeeper complained about the quality and a sample was duly analysed. This found no pollution but some sediment which was deemed responsible for the water appearing dirty, and repairs were ordered to the well covering.

Edwin Rose's salary was the same as his predecessor to start with, the lodge to live in and £25 per annum, but as time passed and the workload grew he several times requested an increase. This was generally granted, though not always as much as he asked for, and in 1877 was accompanied by the reminder that he was to give all his time to the cemetery in the summer and could only do other work in the winter if his duties as lodgekeeper were not neglected. By 1887 the sum was £70 a year. He also earned about £10 a year for digging graves, a small amount for washing the surplice belonging to the Burial Board, plus extra for tasks such as cutting down trees, but the total seems to have been insufficient for him to keep his family. The minute books contain various complaints about him soliciting orders for gravestones for a commission or selling items such as grass and flints from the cemetery, and in April 1890 the Board sternly resolved that if he did anything similar he would be dismissed. He obviously mended his ways sufficiently for this threat not to be enforced as he stayed in his post for several more years.

The lodgekeeper's duties included the care of the paths, grass and shrubs in both the cemetery and the old churchyard. Before the lodge was built the Board had employed a gardener to do this work. The first was George Hinxman of Fisherton Anger who was appointed on 11 June 1856 at a salary of £20 per annum. To begin with he was only responsible for the cemetery but following a vestry meeting in 1858 [6] the Burial Board were requested to take over the care of the old churchyard. Caring for this caused the Board considerable time and expense, especially as the land nearby was developed but they never took the seemingly logical step of appointing a different person to be responsible for it.

There was a change of personnel in 1861 when the Board received an offer from George Smith of Fisherton, gardener, to keep the cemetery in order for £15 a year. Thinking to save money they gave notice to Mr Hinxman and invited tenders but only Mr Smith responded, with a quote for £20 per annum not £15. They accepted his bid, but the attempt had actually lost money as they had to pay for the advert in the local paper.[7] Two years later Mr Smith undertook to keep the old churchyard in order for an additional £4 per annum, and continued in both posts until a lodgekeeper was appointed.

Obviously the initial difficulties caused by shortage of water, which had led to about a third of the original planting dying within a few months, were rapidly overcome. In December 1859 the Board decided that 'the trees and shrubs at the Cemetery having become too much crowded several of them [are] to be removed to the old churchyard.' Three years later they resolved that no more trees or shrubs could be planted by relatives and directed the gardener to prepare the surplus for sale in the autumn, receiving the sum of £11 15s 9d for them.[8] There are regular payments for seeds, flowers and loads of manure, and occasional exceptional ones such as the removal of an Austrian pine tree in 1884.

As time passed the lodgekeeper must have had less and less time for gardening. In July 1872 there was a another complaint that the grass was too long, and he was ordered to keep it shorter. The Board did at least authorise him to get a new scythe to do the job. A year later they considered purchasing an American mowing machine, but after inspecting it decided it was 'inexpedient'. In June 1882 they accepted Mr Foley's offer of the use of his own mowing machine and were presumably favourably impressed as in September they authorised the purchase of one costing £4 10s 0d from Brittan & Sons, nurserymen of Fisherton.

The abundant trees, shrubs and flowerbeds, together with the curving paths as shown on the original plans caused difficulties in locating grave spaces. The situation was complicated by the non rectangular shape of the ground and the numbering system at first adopted by the Board. This meant that regardless of where they were located the plots were simply numbered as they were used, with each space described as lying between sets of hypothetical lines across the cemetery. The Board tackled the issue by directing that numerals be painted on the inside of the walls – presumably to show the 'line' numbers – and by ordering indicators to mark individual grave spaces. At first these were of stone, provided by a Fisherton mason, James Mead, but then 500 pottery ones were ordered from Benjamin Looker, of Norbiton Pottery, Kingston on Thames, which at 4½d each were half the price of the local product.

Grave indicators are a recurrent theme over the years. There were conflicting views about how the markers should be installed – above ground so they could be easily seen (1864) or below the turf so the grass could be cut more easily (1877). Further supplies were ordered from Mr Looker in 1859, 1862 and 1871 before the Board switched back to stone ones, provided at first by Thomas Parkes Lilly, quarry owner of Gillingham, Dorset and then by local masons, Charles James Adey and Edward Tabor.

While the provision of grave markers simplified the task of finding a particular plot there were soon signs that all the trees, shrubs and flower beds were contributing to a second problem, a lack of burial space. The

questionnaire completed when the cemetery was planned had stated that the population it was to serve was 1905 and the average death rate 68 per year but as the population of Fisherton steadily increased (to 4,783 by 1881)[9] the numbers rose. The problem may have started as early as 1862 when the Board directed that any space at least three feet in length should be identified and marked. Two years later they ordered the width of the carriage road on the west side to be reduced to five feet, the same as that on the east.

In spite of the opening of the county lunatic asylum at Devizes in 1852 many pauper patients were cared for and subsequently died at Fisherton House Asylum. The Asylum took large numbers from places such as Portsmouth and London which had insufficient accommodation of their own[10] and together with criminal lunatics these were rapidly filling up Fisherton's smart new cemetery. This situation seems to have been responsible for a cooling of relations between the Finch family and the Burial Board. The land for the original part of the cemetery had been sold by Charles H M Finch, who served as a Board member from its inception in 1854 until 1859. Dr William C Finch was also one of the original members and continued until shortly

A batch of 514 'No 2H' Indicators, numbering 1487-2000 were ordered in 1871

before his death in 1867. William Corbin Finch succeeded his father but only for one three year term, standing down in July 1869 by which time the space shortage was an obvious problem.

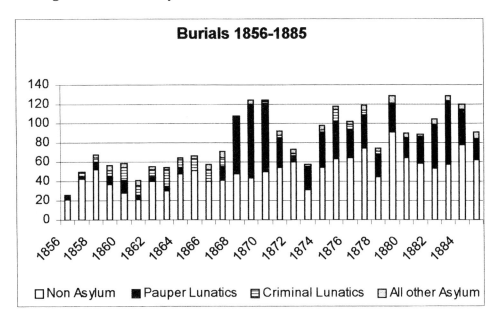

Burials 1856-1885

□ Non Asylum   ■ Pauper Lunatics   ▤ Criminal Lunatics   ▨ All other Asylum

In February 1870 the sexton reported that grave spaces were becoming scarce. Although re-use of spaces after a certain time was permitted there had not been a long enough interval for this to occur at the cemetery. To ease the situation the Board applied to the Secretary of State for permission to inter several pauper patients from the asylum or infirmary in the same space. Their request prompted a visit from the Home Office Inspector of Burial Grounds who suggested they should write to the proprietors of the Asylum. The letter asked for three quarters of an acre adjoining the cemetery free of charge as compensation for the ground already occupied by people from the Asylum and that needed for future plots.

Drs Finch and Lush rejected the Board's request in no uncertain terms, claiming that the number of pauper patient deaths should soon decrease and stating that as substantial ratepayers 'it is not fair to call upon us to provide additional burial space for the use of the parish for all times, more especially when the advantage of the expenditure of the Asylum is considered.' They also felt that a re-arrangement of the space available would avoid the need for any more ground.[11]

In spite of carrying out the re-arrangement of grave spaces as suggested and getting permission for multiple interment of pauper patients (eventually four per grave) the problem soon recurred. In 1875 they again asked Mr Finch to part with some land, this time offering to pay for it. He once more refused so they turned to Lord Pembroke who owned the land on the other side of the cemetery. This too was unsuccessful so they struggled on for a few more years re-using old grave spaces occupied by pauper lunatics and utilising areas allocated as flower beds on the original plan. By the 1880s the situation was critical and at the start of 1883 the Board approached Dr Finch again. It was September before they received a letter from him reluctantly agreeing to sell two acres adjacent to the cemetery but asking 'double the value of the land'. Since this turned out to be £1000 per acre it was far too expensive. After considering a piece of land opposite the cemetery another approach was made to Lord Pembroke.

This time they were successful with his lordship agreeing to sell them two acres on the other side of what is now known as Folly Lane for the very reasonable sum of £100 per acre. They also had to pay £30 to Silas Taunton, Lord Pembroke's tenant farmer, for his trouble in vacating the land. As good public officials the Board felt obliged to check his lordship's title to the land. Unfortunately the first attempt failed with Messrs Purkis & Co of Lincolns Inn Fields, London admitting that although they had seen the patent roll of Henry VIII 'which we should think is a mile long' they could not read it 'in consequence of the abbreviations & writing'.[12] Having arranged for an expert to examine it they were able to confirm that the area in question formed part of the estate granted by the King in 1544 along with the house and the site of the lately dissolved monastery at Wilton.

Fred Bath of Salisbury was selected as architect for the extension and estimated that the costs would be just under £1500, an amount authorised by the vestry. As the site was conveniently adjacent to the existing cemetery expenditure could be minimised because no buildings were needed. A path across the unconsecrated section and a gate in the side wall would provide

The gate between Folly Lane and the original part of the cemetery.

access between the chapels and the new ground. The walls were to be made using local bricks in a similar style to the existing section. Together with the entrance gates they were constructed by Edward Hale of Salisbury at an estimated cost of £630. This time more attention was paid to practical matters. The new ground was an oblong divided into four sections by central paths across width and length, thus maximising the areas available for burials. Three sections were to be consecrated, the type of ground in most demand. Shrubs etc were confined to the central area, around the gates, and along the walls. A detailed planting scheme survives but as no photographs have been found so far it is not possible to determine whether this was followed exactly. Edward John Brittan, nurseryman, of Fisherton Anger, cleared and laid out the new ground as well as constructing paths and planting the trees and shrubs, with his estimate coming to £235. Altogether the work took just under a year and the new ground was consecrated in 13 May 1885. It seems to have been a relatively low key occasion though the parish clerk and Fisherton church choir were in attendance 'together with a fairly large assembly of other friends'.[13] An unusual touch was that the service was conducted by James Butler Kelly, Bishop of Newfoundland, due to the failing health of Bishop Moberly.

Steps were taken to minimise the problems caused by pauper patients from the Asylum, who still came in significant numbers in spite of Dr Finch's assurance that they should diminish, by restricting the area to be used for them to the lower part of the ground furthest from Devizes Road, and by digging deep graves to take four interments. With the opening of the extension the lodge-keeper was responsible for four and a half acres of ground at the cemetery plus the old churchyard, thus it is not surprising that he was reprimanded at various times for failing to keep one or the other site in better order. Routine matters such as repairs and maintenance, approval of all gravestones and inscriptions, requests to purchase grave spaces and replacement of tools and equipment were constant tasks for the Board. On occasion there were more unusual requests to consider such as the application in 1868 from P A Seddon of St Osmund's for a piece of land where Roman Catholics could be buried. The Board refused and it was not until many years later that such a section was created.

In 1895 there was a change in administrative arrangements following the 1894 Parish Councils and District Councils Act.[14] The Act transferred responsibility for secular matters (including cemeteries set up under the Burial Acts) from vestries to the new authorities. The matter was complicated by the fact that the parish of Fisherton Anger lay partly within and partly outside the Borough boundary. The new board met six times a year and its meetings were open to the Press. It had nine members, three more than previously, of whom six were appointed each November by Salisbury Town Council and three each spring at the annual meeting of Fisherton Anger Without Parish Council. Two of the

Fisherton members had previously served on the Board, as had some of the Town Council appointees, and the existing Treasurer and Clerk were confirmed in post, thus providing some continuity of personnel.

The Clerk, George Smith, also Registrar of Burials, had acted for the Board since 1856. His original salary of £15 per annum was increasingly inadequate as the number of burials grew and by 1876 the Vestry finally approved an extra £5 a year for acting as Registrar. He continued to receive this amount plus £5 for the use of his office until his death in 1895, shortly after the new Board was formed. Mr Smith was also Clerk to the Board of the Salisbury Cemetery and his funeral at London Road cemetery was attended by various civic personnel. His replacement was William Charles Powning whose appointment, starting 28 October, was an annual one. His annual salary of £25 included provision of a suitable office which had to be open 10–4 Monday to Friday and 10–2 on Saturdays.

The new Board appointed a smaller Supervisory Committee to oversee routine matters such as approval of memorial inscriptions, with authority to spend sums not exceeding £5. During their first year the Committee seem to have thoroughly inspected all aspects of the cemetery. They advised various maintenance work such as redecorating the sitting room and scullery at the lodge, repainting the chapels doors, front railings and notice boards. A new stove was purchased for the Lodge and six iron seats, eight feet long, were ordered for use by visitors to the cemetery. No major building work took place in the decade after 1895, but there were changes at the chapels. The consecrated chapel door within the porch was replaced by double doors at the outside entrance and both chapels were fitted with some kind of matting. The braziers used for heating were replaced by oil stoves, with the lodgekeeper responsible for providing the necessary oil, wicks, chimneys etc for them.

Although changes to the layout had been made to increase the amount of burial space available, the idea of the garden cemetery with plentiful trees, shrubs and flowers had not been forgotten. In the spring of 1898 the board asked the lodgekeeper to provide a list of he number and kinds of flowers required 'in order that a better display may be made' and authorised expenditure of a sum not exceeding £10. The money was obviously well spent as in August the Supervisory Committee reported that 'the display of Flowers in the Borders is much more satisfactory than last year, the large borders in the new portion of the Cemetery presenting a very good appearance.' Later that year they agreed the spending of 30 shillings on bulbs and wallflowers, with similar payments following for several years. In 1902 details of the plants supplied are given – 240 geraniums, 100 marigolds, about 600 lobelias, plus stocks, asters, blue ageratum, helichrysum, antirrhinum and pansies.

Looking after the flower beds was just one of the lodgekeeper's many duties and perhaps the additional planting to be tended in the new extension was one task too many, or possibly he was simply finding the work too much for him. In June 1900 he was reprimanded for the state of the grass and requested to direct 'his serious attention thereto, failing which the necessity of determining his engagement will have to be considered'. In spite of some improvement a further rebuke followed in August, although this time some practical assistance in the shape of a new mowing machine was offered. Another reprimand was given the following year and in June 1903 he tendered his resignation 'owing to my wife's bad health'. He left at the end of September having completed 28 years at the cemetery, thoughtfully moving out a couple of weeks early so that the lodge could be prepared for the next occupant. There were 40 applicants for the post, four of whom were invited to attend a Board meeting. The successful candidate was Frank Coombs, gardener at Wilbury House Gardens. His salary was the same as his predecessor, the Lodge to live in and £70 a year. His duties were also similar, though those specified make no mention of care of the old churchyard.

With the opening of the new part of the the cemetery in 1885 over 1500 burial spaces were provided, most of them in consecrated ground. However, by 1902 the Board were considering the need for a further extension and had without success approached Lord Pembroke about selling land south of the new section. By October the next year the clerk reported that only 62 consecrated spaces remained in the new ground but that a large part of Section D had not been used and could be consecrated. Approval from the Secretary of State for the alteration was obtained and arrangements made for the consecration on 25 March 1904. Mr Harding, the organist from St Paul's, together with choir members and volunteer helpers attended, but not many members of the general public 'owing, doubtless, to the rather inclement weather'.[15] Satisfaction with the new piece of consecrated ground must have been marred by the death a few days later of the Clerk, William C Powning. Mr George J Henbest (who had been Acting Clerk before Mr Powning was appointed) was chosen to succeed him, to commence on 11 May with duties and salary the same as his predecessor.

When the cemetery had opened in 1856 it had been very isolated, but as time passed houses gradually came closer. By 1897 the Burial Board noted that there was an adequate footpath almost all the way to the cemetery, only the last stretch from Dr Finch's lodge (now India Avenue) being unsatisfactory. They complained to Wilton District Council who promised to carry out the work and by February 1898 were able to record that 'an excellent Footpath' had been provided for the final section. This joining of the city centre and the cemetery seems symbolic of the diminishing independence of Fisherton Anger and the growth of Salisbury, a situation which intensified in December 1903 when the Board received notice that the Town Council planned an alteration to the city boundaries. Fisherton Anger Without the Borough was among the areas proposed for inclusion in the expanded city. The Board unanimously approved of the proposed extension which after a Local Government Board enquiry came into effect in November the next year.

The Burial Board's last meeting was held on 17 October 1904 and was much concerned with horticultural matters. They noted that the newly planted box bushes on either side of the entrance gates to the old part of the cemetery

The Finch family plot (below) with close up of one of the decorative finials (above). The pillar commemorating Arthur Foley (right), who died 5 Dec 1894, and seven members of his family

were a great improvement, recommended that a golden arbor vitae tree be purchased to replace one which had failed, that some privet bushes be planted behind the lodge, and agreed to spend the usual 30 shillings on spring bulbs. They also recorded their appreciation of the services rendered by the retiring members of the Board (those appointed by Fisherton Without Parish Council) – Rev E Thwaites, member since 1874, Robert C Harding, member from 1880, and Thomas Perkins, member from 1895.

Thus ended the separate existence of Fisherton cemetery's Burial Board. Under the new arrangements the Town Council was also the Burial Board and as such decided that there should be quarterly general meetings with monthly meetings of the two cemetery management committees. Mr Henbest was appointed Clerk to the new board at a salary of £85 per year with an allowance of £10 for an office, and by the end of December was established in new premises at Crown Chambers, Bridge Street.[16] Many of those associated with the cemetery were eventually laid to rest there, including Mr Henbest himself, Robert Curtis Harding and Arthur Foley (Board members) and several members of the Finch family.

The history of the creation of Fisherton cemetery can be found in the first issue of Sarum Chronicle, *2001, back issues still available.*

References

Documents relating to Fisherton Anger (FA) cemetery have been deposited with the Wiltshire & Swindon Record Office.

G23/207/1-4 FA cemetery loose papers (including Contract Book) 1855-1904

G23/200/1 FA Burial Board minutes 1854-85

G23/200/2 FA Burial Board minutes 1885-95

G23/200/3 FA Burial Board minutes 1895-1904

also: 2561/6 FA vestry minutes 1855-90

2561/12 FA parish magazine 1895

Salisbury & Winchester Journal (*SJL*)

Salisbury Times (*STM*)

1 *SJL* 26 Apl 1856, p3
2 Contract Book 46-56. Walls: of brick and flint with stone quoins
3 *SJL* 22 Sep 1866, p5
4 RG10/1957/folio 24
5 RG11/2073 folio 15
6 Vestry mins 5 Aug 1858
7 *SJL* 25 May 1861, p5
8 BB mins 1862, 19 Feb, 19 Jne & 3 Sep
9 Vestry mins 17 Feb 1888
10 Chandler, J, *Endless Street*, Hobnob Press, 1987, p226
11 BB mins 9 Jne 1870
12 G23/207/4
13 2561/12, June issue
14 Local Government Act 1894
15 *STM* 1 April 1904, p8
16 *STM* 16 Dec 1904

Photos by author. Finch enclosure 2001, others 2004

The Treasury and Muniment Room at Salisbury Cathedral

Tim Tatton-Brown

A small two-storied octagonal building, made as a treasury/vestry and muniment room, is the only later addition to Salisbury Cathedral. Unlike the cloister and chapter house, which were planned from the beginning, this building was butted up against the south-east side of the south-east transept, and a doorway was cut through the transept south wall from St Nicholas' chapel to allow access. Despite being an afterthought, this building was almost certainly added to this part of the cathedral less than half a century after the original construction, perhaps in the 1250s or 1260s.

The building itself consists of two principal chambers, one above the other, which are both octagonal in plan (and c. 30 feet in diameter). The upper chamber is approached from a fine stone staircase on the west (it is within an enlarged north-west wall and is vaulted above) which runs up to it from the vestibule of the lower chamber. This vestibule (internal dimensions c.15 x 12ft 6in.) connects the lower octagonal chamber with St Nicholas' chapel on the north (now the modern outer vestry). Both its north and south doorways were double (for extra security), and three out of the four wooden doors survive (the northern of the two doors in the south wall is sadly missing). There is another original door into the staircase (which has a unique medieval cogged locking device on its back) and two more at the head of the stairs which still have their bolts. Interestingly they were bolted from the inside in each case. The vestibule has an original fireplace and chimney in its east wall, between two tall rectangular shuttered, windows, and this fireplace was reopened in November 1993. It now contains a modern boiler, but behind and below this survive the herringbone tiles for the fireplace. Above it, is a well-preserved chimney flue. The almost flat roof of this vestibule area was apparently remade in the Scott restoration of the 1860s (it is still lead-covered), and just beneath it are the remains, in the north and south walls, of two bands of typical 13th-century red-painted decoration. A new raised timber-floor was apparently put into this vestibule in 1956. No tile-pavement seems to exist beneath it.

Exterior of the Treasury and Muniment Room from the south-west

The ground floor octagonal chamber has now been completely refurnished, so it is difficult to make out many of the original features. A little bit of the red-painted false ashlar decoration is, however, visible in some of the window embrasures, and some shutters can also be seen. In the centre of the room is the original Purbeck marble shaft and capital (the base is hidden beneath desks), which are joined together by an iron clamp (with lead run into the joint from two holes on the north and south sides of the capital). It now supports a massive north-west to south-east oak composite tie-beam, which was entirely renewed in 1931-2. The ends of the tie-beam sit on stone corbels in the wall. There are five rectangular windows (arched over on the outside) lighting the room, which were all at first shuttered internally. Externally the windows were heavily barred, but all the outer bars were cut off in the 19th-century restorations. The inner iron window bars do, however, survive. The outside wall-face of the building has also been heavily refaced and repointed (with new ventilation grills, in the form of large 'M's added). The original medieval face is not of ashlar, but of coursed flint with masonry side-alternate angle quoins. Until c1790 there was also a small rectangular two-storied

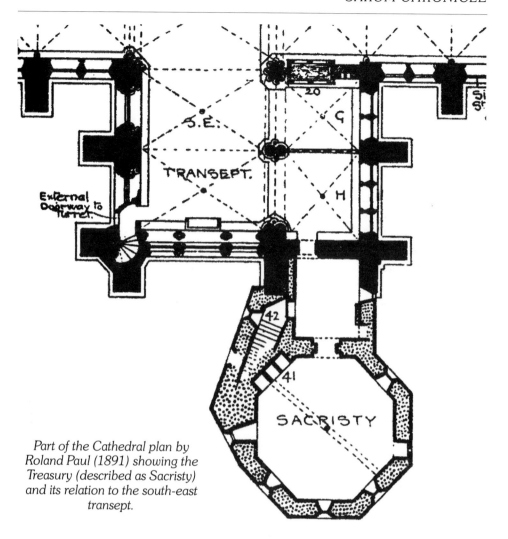

Part of the Cathedral plan by Roland Paul (1891) showing the Treasury (described as Sacristy) and its relation to the south-east transept.

building on the east side of the octagon, which may once have been used as the living chambers for the sub-treasurer, and it was probably he who had to bolt the doors from the inside at night. Inside both the ground-floor chamber and the upper chamber are blocked-up doorways to this extension (in the east wall). To the north of the ground-floor doorway was a fine late-medieval lavabo, which was relocated to the Morning Chapel (north-east transept, near the font) in the 19th century. In the north-west wall are three deep wall-cupboards (aumbries), with modern doors, and there is another smaller wall-cupboard a little further to the south. This room was refurbished some years ago as the main inner vestry (and office for the vergers), and it is not known whether it originally had a tiled floor beneath its modern wood-floor.

The first-floor octagonal chamber above was almost certainly used as a muniment room from soon after its construction until it was converted into the choir-practice room in the early 1970s (i.e. for *c*700 years). This exceptional space was first depicted, and quaintly described, by the Rev Peter Hall in his *Picturesque Memorials of Salisbury* (1834), though he does not mention the magnificent tile pavement (see below). The room was visibly little changed 125 years later when Hugh Shortt described it, and the tile pavement, in the 31st *Annual Report of the Cathedral Friends* (1961). The roof had, by this time, been completely rebuilt in 1931-2 (see below). As Hall's 1834 engraving shows, the room contained a series of large medieval chests (many of them covered in iron, and having many locks) and cupboards. There were also some wooden benches, and a long table on which stood the Dean and Chapter's seal-press, and it was here that one came to look at, and handle, the cathedral's copy of Magna Carta. On either side of the central post were two large iron-bound chests, the larger of which was so heavy that its lid had to be opened by a pulley and small windlass attached to the central post. The three largest chests are now in the north choir aisle while the smallest is still *in situ*, chained to the wall. On the north-west side of the room is an exceptionally important muniment cupboard (or *armoire*), which almost certainly dates from the 14th century.

The present roof was constructed in 1931-2, but is a replica of the original, as Hall's 1834 engraving shows. A drawn section through the roof and

Peter Hall's engraving (published 1834) of the Muniment Room

central post is in Cecil Hewett's book *English Cathedral and Monastic Carpentry* (1985), fig. 100, and Hewett describes the roof thus:

> It is an octagon with straight rafters for eight triangles, and the central pier has an elaborately-carved capital and stop-chamfered brace, and the wall-posts stand upon stone corbels. There are eight double principal-rafters with trapped purlins and common-rafters.

The roof was until 1932 covered in lead, when it was replaced by copper. Access to the roof is by a small spiral stair to a turret, from a doorway in the north-west corner of the room. The turret is polygonal in form above the roof and parapet, and still has its original wooden (and lead-covered) roof, with a moulded cornice. The door from the roof on to the turret is also original. Until just over thirty years ago the inside walls of the upper chamber were almost entirely covered with 13th-century red-painted decoration, with a scroll pattern at the top, and red-lined false ashlar down to a double line at the top of the dado. Most unfortunately this has all been covered in limewash, except for a small section of the scroll pattern over the entrance doorway. The five original shutters for the windows have recently been reinstated, after having for a time been removed from their hooks, and put in a pile on top of a cupboard.

The pavement of the room is now, of course, the most important surviving original feature and this, and its tiles, have already been fully discussed by Dr Christopher Norton for the *British Archaeological Association Salisbury Conference Transactions* (1996, 90-105). It is the only *in situ* medieval tile pavement in England to survive at first floor level, not on a stone vault. The tiles rest on a mortar bed, which sits on a 1932 floor of sawn planks on a series of tie-beams, which, in turn, sit on the large north-west to south-east cross-beam already mentioned. Most unfortunately all the woodwork was replaced in 1931-2, and as a result the tile pavement has been settling down over the new timbers for the last seventy or so years. Most of the tiles around the edge of the pavement have also pulled away from the plaster wall-face, leaving large gaps.

W A Forsyth, the consulting architect for Salisbury Cathedral from 1921-40 says in his final report (dated 2 December 1940) that:

> In 1931 the roof and the supporting timbers of the famous 14th-century tiled floor of the Muniment Room were found to be seriously attacked by the 'Death Watch' beetle to such an extent as to endanger the use of the Vestry below. The roof was of oak construction covered with cast lead. The main timbers, the wall plates and the great centre post were in an advanced state of decay. The tiled floor, supported on oak slabs forming the ceiling of the Vestry, was in danger of collapse.

Forsyth then goes on to describe how work was carried out between November 1931 and May 1932 on the replacement of all the defective oak rafters, beams and other roof members, and notes that, 'the renewal of the oak slabs and beams supporting the tile floor was most skilfully undertaken without disturbing the tiles'.

He also describes the replacement of all the lead covering of the gutters and the roof with copper, which he says was a much better material being less subject to expansion and only one-eighth of the weight of lead! 'It also produces a poison in the condensation on the underside which should destroy the fungus from which the 'Death Watch' beetle is said to derive its food, should an attack recur.' The cost of all these works was £1,460 5s 5d.

In 1969 it was decided to turn the Muniment Room into the choir-practice room, and the table and large chests were removed. The tiled floor was covered and a grand piano was brought in, as well as the cupboards and furnishings from the old song school. It was at this time apparently that the walls were whitewashed, and the five original shutters taken off their hooks and stored, to allow more light to enter the room. Since 1970 the room has been used every day as a choir practice room. It also houses the music library.

Where was Old Sarum?

John Chandler

Where was Old Sarum? So simple a question has a simple answer only if, by Old Sarum, one is referring to the Iron Age hillfort, the Norman castle, or its adjunct, Salisbury's first cathedral. The Roman town of Old Sarum (if such it was), *Sorviodunum*, is being shown from an accumulation of archaeological evidence to have been a nebulous affair, embracing not only the fortified hilltop, but also the high ground of Paul's Dene towards Bishopsdown, land around and behind the Old Castle Inn, and (principally) much of present-day Stratford-sub-Castle, extending down to and across the River Avon.[1] The medieval town of Old Sarum is similarly perplexing, and this paper seeks to draw together some strands of evidence about its nature and whereabouts.

Until the mid-20th century it was assumed that much, if not all, of the medieval town lay within the hillfort, and that development outside was suburban.[2] This view has occasionally been championed more recently,[3] but excavations during the 1950s and 1960s, and the publication of a detailed history of Old Sarum by Sir Francis Hill,[4] convinced most researchers that the nucleus of the town lay outside the hillfort's east gate.[5] An increasing body of archaeological evidence (including recent and as yet unpublished excavations) confirms this view.[6]

That some form of extra-mural settlement extended from this nucleus down the Portway towards the river was implicit in the practice of holding elections to the borough in this area at the 'Parliament Tree'.[7] A sketch plan in Salisbury Museum of about 1700 or a little earlier (Figure 1) depicts burgage plots of various widths lining both sides of the Portway from the hillfort to the river.[8] This plan (alongside other evidence) was noted by Maurice Beresford, in his classic study of town plantation, who included Old Sarum, somewhat equivocally, in his gazetteer of English new towns.[9]

Although the sketch plan is too rough for topographical accuracy, it has been noticed that greater precision can be achieved by examining the Stratford-sub-Castle enclosure and tithe maps, of 1800 and 1839 respectively (WSRO EA74; T/A Stratford), and identifying lands formerly in lay, rather than ecclesiastical, ownership. These, it was maintained, undoubtedly represented the borough lands, which were concentrated in the town's nucleus around the Old Castle Inn (described above) and along the Portway.[10]

A rather better indicator of the former borough lands can be found in fact by plotting all land parcels recorded on the tithe apportionment as paying tithe to the Prebendary of Stratford rather than to the Dean and Chapter. These comprise a series of rectangular blocks bordering the Portway, and extending northwards towards the hillfort's east gate. Confirmation that these are indeed the borough lands comes in an 18th-century copy of the 1649 survey of church lands preserved among the chapter records.[11] The 1649 survey runs as follows:

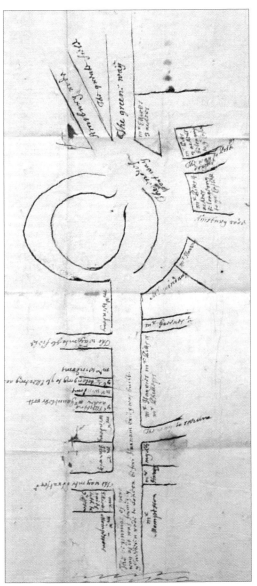

> There belongs also to the said Prebend the tythe of 2 furlongs of arrable land lying within the parish of Stratford aforesaid, the one lying in the home field the other in the South field, each of them abutting upon the highway called the Portway, which furlongs contain of estimation seventy acres, and also the tithe of a certain meadow . . . called Kingsbridge Meade containing by estimation 4 acres. . .

This 18th-century copy has a marginal note against the 70 acres:

> These 2 furlongs comprehend all the Burrough lands and extend on the South field from the upper end of Portway down to Edmond's Garden inclusive, and from the Castle wall in Homefield to the Street: the crofts called Harvys alias Harvest Crofts inclusive.

Figure 1 Sketch map of about 1700 showing electoral burgage plots (Salisbury & South Wilts Museum PD 33997)

By the 19th century, when the enclosure and tithe maps were drawn up, much consolidation of landholdings in Stratford had taken

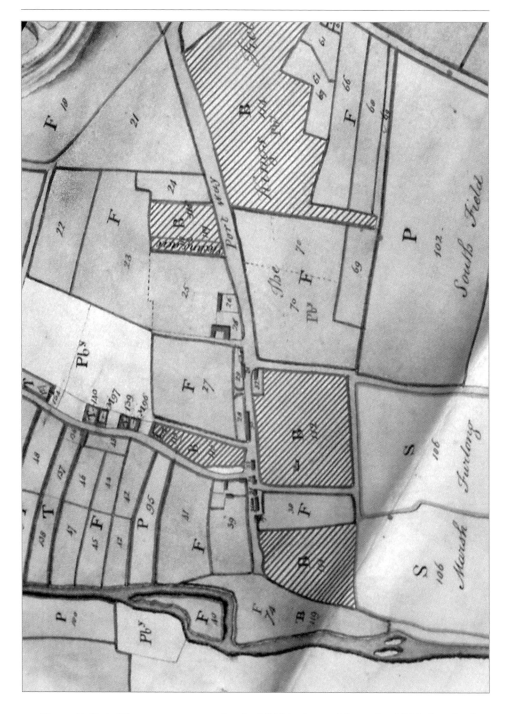

Figure 2 Detail from a map on a deed of 1804, derived from the 1793 Stratford estate map (WSRO CC Chapter 14/3). Part of the ramparts of Old Sarum hillfort can be seen in the top left hand corner; the River Avon runs along the foot of the map.

place and many field boundaries had been lost. Fortunately, however, a slightly earlier map with more boundaries has survived among the Church Commissioners' records, surveyed by Webb and Tubb of Salisbury in 1793, and annexed to a deed of 1802.[12] It formed the basis for (or is otherwise related to) three other maps annexed to deeds in the same bundle of 1804 (Figure 2), 1818 and 1820. This family of maps, taken with the tithe and enclosure maps already referred to, and an estate catalogue map of 1849,[13] makes it possible to plot, with a better chance of topographical accuracy, the field layout just prior to enclosure, and to superimpose on it the extent of the two furlongs, tithable to the prebend, described in 1649, which were believed in the 18th century to comprise the borough of Old Sarum (Figure 3).

The regularity of the resulting plan, which shows surviving rectangular burgages running back to straight rear boundaries flanking a broad spinal street, leaves little doubt that, on topographical grounds at least, here is cartographic and documentary evidence of a planted medieval town, or (perhaps more accurately) a very large planned extension to an existing town. It shows, furthermore, that the topography of present-day Stratford-sub-Castle, especially the two right-angled bends in Stratford Road, is a consequence of the town plan, and that a significant portion of Stratford village overlies it.[14]

Apart from the Portway itself and some surviving boundaries there appear to be no extant earthworks or archaeological features of the former town visible on the ground or from the air. Small-scale and piecemeal excavations in the area have recovered evidence for three or four medieval buildings, but not the quantity of occupation remains which might be expected in an urban context.[15] It is worth noting, however, that during the 18th century, when much of the site was under arable cultivation, cropmarks of something were visible. In a speech delivered in February 1780 Edmund Burke alluded to Old Sarum, which:

> was once a place of trade, and sounding with the busy hum of men, though now you can only trace the streets by the colour of the corn, and its sole manufacture is in members of Parliament.[16]

This planned settlement below Old Sarum may be compared with many similar developments of the 12th and 13th centuries elsewhere, including locally the bishop of Winchester's plantations at Downton and Alresford, and the bishop of Salisbury's own plantation of Sherborne Newland.[17] Seen in a national context it bears an uncanny resemblance to the plan of Brinklow, Warwickshire, and stands comparison with many towns (eg Olney and Eynsham) described by Beresford.[18] It has affinities also with two major cities which received cathedrals adjacent to castles at the same time as Old Sarum – Lincoln and Norwich.

Beresford's ground-breaking study was not available when Hill published his work on Old Sarum in 1962, but some of the information he provided has an immediate resonance to anyone familiar with that work, or with the many studies of individual towns published subsequently.[19] Hill found the name 'Newton Westgate' in 1353 and 1424, and an aldermanry named Newton in 1361, both of which he suggested might have referred to the Portway and its settlement. The latter reference, which had been noted by Hatcher in 1843, derives from the will of John atte Stone, who owned, 'one messuage and one croft of arable land . . . in the aldermanry of Newton adjacent to (*desuper*) the castle'.[20]

Although the name Newton was often applied generally to a new farm or minor settlement, in an urban context Newport and Newton / Newtown were names by which planted towns were frequently known. Beresford's gazetteer includes no fewer than eight instances in southern England between Devon and the Isle of Wight.[21] The affix 'Westgate', presumably referring to its position at the western approach to the town of Old Sarum,[22] may have been applied to distinguish it from other nearby Newtons – Newton Tony, South Newton and Newtown (in Durnford).

Unlike New Sarum (the modern Salisbury), which was established by, and on land belonging to, the bishops of Salisbury, Old Sarum belonged to the Crown, and the town there was a royal borough. It was, however, surrounded by the large rural estate known as Salisbury, or the Salisburies, which was episcopal property, and bishop Osmund granted parts of it to endow his chapter and individual prebends in Old Sarum cathedral. If Newton is identifiable as the planted settlement astride the Portway then on the evidence of both its name and its topography it is a later phase of development than the town clustered outside the castle's east gate. But it is probably not much later. To extend his town and build Newton the king, one assumes, would have needed to take land belonging to the bishop, but of this there appears to be no documentary record.

This suggests that, like other plantations adjacent to castles, Newton was established quite early in the Norman period, before the downfall of bishop Roger in 1139 heralded the divorce between church and state at Old Sarum. Although no evidence has been found to give Roger the credit, it is perhaps most likely that Newton was established by him. He was investing heavily in work on Old Sarum castle and cathedral during the 1120s and 1130s, when he had effective control of both, as well as the town; and it was at about this period (during the reign of Henry I, 1100-1130) that Old Sarum received its first charter, granting it a market, privileges and a merchant guild.

Furthermore Roger during his lifetime attained a reputation as a lavish and enterprising builder of castles, churches and houses. His principal estates lay within the counties of his diocese (Berkshire, Dorset and Wiltshire) and he was ranked among the wealthiest of 12th-century magnates.[23] His activities as a town founder and planner are shadowy and have not received much attention, but it is possible that he was responsible for urban development at Wokingham on his manor of Sonning, a realignment of the street pattern at Sherborne, and the

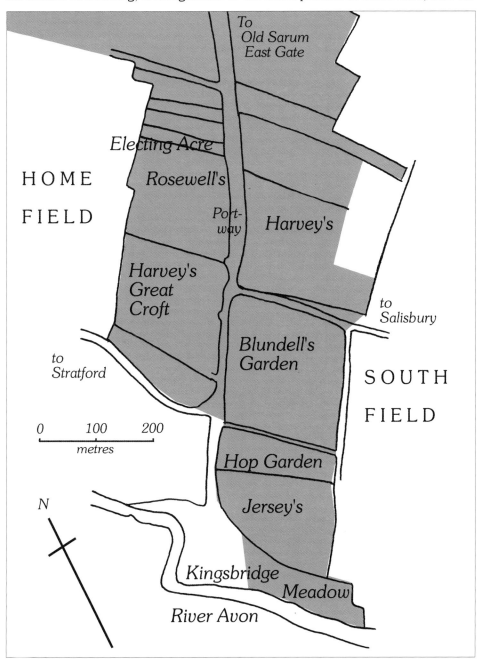

Figure 3 Boundaries and some names derived from 1793 estate map and derivatives. The area shaded grey approximates to land parcels tithable to the Prebend of Stratford in 1839, and gives an indication of former borough lands.

establishment of twin planted settlements beside his new castle at Kidwelly in south Wales.[24] At Malmesbury, where Roger built a castle, he may also have constructed the town's wall, and it is an intriguing speculation that he could have been responsible for developing the suburb of Westport (first recorded by name in 1135 and with a guildhall by *c* 1200) as a planned extension to the town.[25] Closer to home he initiated, or more likely continued the work of his predecessor Osmund in initiating, the town planted at Devizes outside the castle.[26]

It has been noted above that evidence for the existence of burgages on either side of the Portway owes its survival to their significance for electing members to the 'rotten' Parliamentary borough of Old Sarum. If, as is often claimed, Old Sarum was rapidly deserted during the 13th century in favour of New Sarum, it is hard to understand why it was called to send burgesses to the 'model' Parliament of 1295, and to elect representatives in 1361 and thereafter.[27] Its ecclesiastical and diocesan functions ceased, of course, and with them all trade and income derived from churchmen and pilgrims. But the castle continued to provide work for Old Sarum tradesmen until the 1360s at least. The trappings of urban life continued, too, though scaled down, with a three-day fair granted in 1246, taxation as a borough until 1336 and reference to a mayor as late as 1453.[28] John Leland, visiting in 1542, was assured that houses had existed in what he described as the east suburb within living memory.[29] But where was this Old Sarum? The evidence surviving of the procedures for electing to the 'rotten borough' suggests that borough life continued, not on Cobbett's 'accursed hill', but outside and below, especially at Newton along the Portway.

The suspicion that a medieval planted town, Newton, was established below Old Sarum castle in the 12th century, and that it continued to function as a major element in the borough of Old Sarum after the hilltop became uninhabited in the 13th, should lead to a reassessment of a number of traditional views. The name 'Stratford', for instance, is generally derived from the river-crossing of the Roman road leading to Dorchester, close to the line of the Portway. But if this area was called Newton in the 12th century, then presumably Stratford referred to another Roman river crossing further upstream, close to the present parish church of St Laurence, which carried the road (lost in this vicinity) through Grovely to the Mendips.

A second misapprehension would be that upon its creation New Sarum was populated by economic migrants, as they would now be termed, pouring down from the barren and inhospitable hilltop town of Old Sarum. Many would merely be exchanging life beside a river in one planted town (barely a century old) for life in another, further downstream.

A third fallacy would then be that Old Sarum is or was ever deserted. The borough, so far as it continued to operate after the 13th-century exodus (and like its Roman precursor), may have been centred on what has become Stratford-sub-Castle, where Stratford Road makes its two right-angled turns. Old Sarum then becomes a matter, not of medieval extinction, but of medieval rebranding.[30]

Notes

1 James, David J, 2002, Sorviodunum: a review of the archaeological evidence. *WANHM*, 95, 1-26; Corney, Mark, 2001, The Romano-British nucleated settlements of Wiltshire. In Ellis, P (ed.), *Roman Wiltshire and after* (Devizes: WANHS), 5-38, on 18-23)

2 eg Braun, Hugh, 1960, The earthworks of Old Sarum. *WANHM* 57, 406-7

3 eg Stroud, Daphne, 1986, The site of the borough of Old Sarum 1066-1226: an examination of some documentary evidence. *WANHM*, 80, 120-6

4 Musty, John and Rahtz, Philip A, 1964, The suburbs of Old Sarum. *WANHM* 59, 130-54; Hill, Sir Francis, 1962, Old Sarum. In Crittall, Elizabeth (ed.), *Victoria History of Wiltshire*, vol. 6, 51-67

5 eg RCHM, 1980, Royal Commission on Historical Monuments, *Salisbury*, vol. 1. London: HMSO; Chandler, John, 1983, *Endless Street: a history of Salisbury and its people*. Salisbury: Hobnob Press, 3, 7-8

6 Listed and described in Old Sarum extensive urban survey, by Bill Moffatt for Wiltshire County Council, in preparation. I am indebted to Roy Canham for giving me access to a draft of this report. The most notable recent discovery (in 2002 and not yet published) has been the probable site and remains of St John's Hospital some 500m east of the hillfort's east gate.

7 Musty, John and Hadley, John D, 1991, Old Sarum and the Parliament Tree. *Hatcher Review* 4 (32), 39-43

8 Salisbury & S. W. Museum, PD 33997; reproduced by Renn, D, 1994, *Old Sarum*. London: English Heritage, 32; and (redrawn) by Hill (*op. cit.*, 66).

9 Beresford, M W, 1967, *New towns of the middle ages: town plantation in England, Wales and Gascony*. London: Lutterworth, 508-9

10 Hill, *op. cit.*, 63; the maps are in WSRO (EA 74; T/A Stratford sub Castle)

11 WSRO CC Chapter 1/1

12 WSRO CC. Chapter 14/2; other deeds and plans also in Chapter, bundle 14.

13 WSRO CC. Maps 48

14 David James has suggested to me the intriguing possibility that these plots may be related to earlier Roman centuriation along the adjacent Roman road.

15 Moffatt (note 6 above), who on this basis rejects the notion that the medieval town extended down the Portway to the river. However, excavation in this area has been very limited, and (for the most part) focussed on discovering evidence of Roman settlement.

16 Magnus, Sir Philip (ed.), 1948, *Selected prose of Edmund Burke*. London: Falcon Press [Speech on the plan for economical reform, 11 February 1780]

17 Beresford, Maurice, 1959, Six new towns of the bishop of Winchester. *Medieval Archaeology* 3, 187-215, ; Penn, K J, 1980, *Historic towns in Dorset*. Dorchester: DNHAS Monograph series 1, 95

18 Lilley, K D, 1993-4, A Warwickshire medieval borough: Brinklow and the contribution of town-plan analysis.

Transactions of the Brimingham and Warwickshire Archaeological Society, 98, 51-60; Beresford, *op. cit.* (1967), *passim*

19 reviewed in Slater, T R, 2000, Understanding the landscape of towns. In Hooke, D (ed.), *Landscape: the richest historical record* (Amesbury: Society for Landscape Studies, supplementary series 1), 97-108

20 Hill *op. cit.*, 64; Hatcher, Henry, 1843, *Old and New Sarum, or Salisbury*, by Robert Benson and Henry Hatcher. London: Nichols, 63; WSRO G23/1/212, f.57

21 Beresford *op. cit.* (1967), 382 (note 6), 390

22 Moffatt (see note 6 above) considers that Newton Westgate related to the (partially extant) rectilinear arrangement of earthworks leading away from the castle west gate, but this is much more likely to have been the canons' gardens and dwellings, on land granted by Osmund in 1091 for this purpose, *ante portam Castelli Seriberiensis terram ex utraque parte vie* ('land before the castle gate of Salisbury on each side of the road'). This identification has been convincingly argued by Stroud *op. cit.*, 124. 'Newton' would hardly be appropriate to such a development.

23 Stalley, R A, 1971, A twelfth-century patron of architecture. *Journal of the British Archaeological Association*, 3rd series, 34, 62-83; Kealey, Edward J, 1972, *Roger of Salisbury: viceroy of England*. Los Angeles: University of California Press, 96-7, 277

24 Wokingham: Beresford *op. cit.* (1967), 396-7; Sherborne: Penn *op. cit.*, 94; Kidwelly: Stalley *op. cit.*; Beresford *op. cit.* (1967), 541

25 Freeman, Jane, 1991, Malmesbury, and Westport. In Crowley, D A (ed.), *Victoria history of Wiltshire*, vol. 14, 127-68, 229-40, on 132, 231

26 Chandler, John, 2003, *Devizes and central Wiltshire*. East Knoyle: Hobnob Press, 46-8

27 Roskill, J S, 1992, *The House of Commons 1386-1421*, vol. 1. Stroud: Alan Sutton (History of Parliament), 710

28 Hill *op. cit.*, 62-3; Roskell, *op. cit.*, 710, 711 note 6

29 Smith, L T (ed.), 1906, *The itinerary of John Leland*, vol. 1. London: Centaur Press [1964 reprint], 261

30 I am most grateful to David James for discussing this research with me; to Jane Standen and Peter Saunders of Salisbury Museum for permitting me to photograph the sketch map of Old Sarum burgages (Figure 1); to the Wiltshire & Swindon Record Office, for access to archives and permission to reproduce the 1804 map (Figure 2); and to Roy Canham and Bill Moffatt for granting me access to the latter's unpublished report (see above, note 6).

The Spinster and the Plague

Steve Hobbs and Sue Johnson

Salisbury has been well served by its historians, but only the most pertinacious of researchers would delve far into the poem that gushed from the pen of 'Miss Child' to produce over 300 pages of doggerel, first published in 1844 as *The Spinster at Home in the Close of Salisbury*. Frankly to modern tastes it is pretty dire; but it was popular in its time and ran to six editions. Buoyed by its success and keen to avoid criticisms of poetic licence, in 1852 Miss Child produced *An Historical Appendix* supporting the veracity of events and individuals mentioned in the poem. She had previously demonstrated her apparent desire for accuracy in a footnote appended to a passage in her sixth edition (published in 1849) which is the subject of this brief paper. For a mere footnote it is quite extravagant, since it continues in small print for much of four pages (359-62). It is also muddle-headed, as the excuse for including it is a reference to the cholera, not the plague:

> *Extracts from the Diary of Anthony Abbott* (A. D. 1627.)
>
> March. This morning cometh the Leech into mine house, and telleth me of a surety the plague hath broken out in this city; and we did debate whether it would be tempting God his providence to remain, seeing that so many of my fellow-citizens, as he informed me, were already preparing to quit their habitations and fly into the country; but forasmuch as the commodities wherein I deal are precious; and great calamities do often breed pillage, and rapine, and all manner of lawlessness, I did finally resolve to stay; whereto my wife did also counsel me.
>
> April 9. To the Poultry Cross, where I did hear a fanatic hold forth. His face was much forpined [wasted away], and his eyes did glare like live coals: the more especially when he did denounce God his judgments upon this sinful city, speaking in a loud voice like one possessed (as truly I do think he was). They which stood by, did tremble as they listened, but presently cometh Master Mayor, which ordered him to be set in the stocks, whereupon the fanatic did call him Armageddon, and did blaspheme mightily, so that he foamed at the mouth.
>
> May. The clergy and them which be about the Cathedral have shut themselves up within the Close, as it were in a besieged city, and we do lack the offices of religion, whereof we have such grievous need, when men be daily dying all around us, and we cannot tell what one among us may he doomed next.

June 16. Woe, woe. The plague hath even made my own house desolate. The wife of my bosom, – she which I did love from my youth upward as though it were my other self, fell sick about four of the clock in the afternoon, and presently the plague-spots did break out about her neck, and death did speedily ensue. Methought as I looked on the purple corpse, and did forecaste [sic, misreading foretaste?] the sad and heavy hours which were to come, I could gladly have died too; and when I did address myself to prayer, the words 'THY WILL BE DONE' did almost choke me in the utterance; whereof my conscience did afterward reprove me.

June 17, 18, 19. In much affliction, so did keep no record.

July 27. The sad spectacle of this silent city sorely grieveth me. There be so many shops and houses closed; some with padlocks on their doors, and others with a red cross painted on the lintel, which doth signify infection. Many of them I did once know, be dead, many more fled into the country, and not a few have barred themselves within doors, having laid up great store of provisions, and let none of their family or servants come in or go forth. Them which do venture abroad, keep to the middle of the street, applying herbs and scents to their nostrils and bestowing careful heed upon their steps, lest unwarily they should encounter one which hath the infection.

Aug. 7.Yesterday I held discourse with a godly woman which the Mayor had appointed to the office of Searcher, which did tell me that about the necks of the poorer sort of people which have died of the plague, philtres, and charms, and amulets were hung; and some had cabalistic characters on slips of Sheep-Skin tied about them – as though such trumpery could save them! She said that it was pitiful to see how that often times the little babe would perish on its mother's breast, and wives would throw themselves upon their husbands, which were dead, and would not suffer any one to tear them away, so that the infection presently seized upon them: and many more particulars she did relate, hard to be believed in a Christian land.

Sept. 12. Truly the stillness of the city is terrible: for no bell knolleth unto church, and men when they do meet speak in whispers, and every day hath verily become a sad and solemn sabbath. Certain of the streets have chains drawn across them, by order of the Mayor, who hath been wonderfully diligent, and hath been miraculously preserved; and I did espy the grass growing on divers of the thresholds. Some of them I did remember right well, and did bethink me with a heavy heart of the summer evenings in former years, when I did use to see young children playing on them, and when I did use to hear the sweet voices of maidens singing at the casements, which be now all boarded up and dark.

Sept. 15. Daily, to my apprehension, the plague doth grow worse; only the watchers with their red staves, and the nurses with their hoods and whimples seem to be abroad, and likewise them which be charged with the distribution of provisions. No manner of merchandize cometh in or goeth out of the city; and they which be appointed to traffic with the country people go forth upon the hills, standing apart from them they barter with; and whatsoever provisions they buy, they cast the money for the same into vessels of vinegar, that the country people may not be affected thereby. All about the outskirts of the city, there be men stationed who suffer none to pass, except them which be permitted by Master Mayor.

Sept. 30. It chanced that as I did pass through Winchester-street, pondering, as I fail not continually to do, upon the mercies which had been vouchsafed to me, my ears were pierced with the howling of a dog, which did crouch within the porchway of a house upon the left hand side as you do go towards the Croft; so, when as I drew near, it ceased, and yet did seem to have a human grief upon its honest face, and meekly fawned upon me, and did lick my hand, looking up at me wistfully and piteously methought. Then I did perceive the door was open, and did hear wailings and childish cries, as it were in an upper chamber, which amazed me greatly, for I did think them to be all dead which did dwell therein. So I did debate whether I should rashly enter therein, or seek out a searcher and incontinently send her thither; but, certes, the dog did seem to penetrate my thoughts, and did run to and fro, like as he would beckon me forward, so I forgat my peril, and did follow my dumb guide, climbing up divers stairs and passing through a dark corridor, until I came into the chamber from which the sounds of lamentation did issue forth: howbeit the pestilent smell of death did somewhat terrify me, so that I did almost repent me of my rashness; natheless I did presently resolve to enter. Upon a fair and stately bed did lay two corpses, and looking thereon I did perceive the buboes, which did denote that they had perished of the plague: they had not long been dead, and them which tended them fled for very fear. But that which did make my heart to bleed was the sad spectacle of two fair children, which did spend their little breath in piercing cries and sobs, because their parents would not waken, and the elder of the twain, which was not aged more than four years, did beseech me in such moving terms that I would waken their mother, for they were fearful and a-hungry, that I was fain to mingle my tears with them which they shed, which did relieve my heart. And forasmuch as I greatly feared lest death should come upon both them and me, I led them forth into mine own house, and by good hap was not questioned of any of the watchers I did meet: and when I arrived there I set forth meat and drink for these poor little ones, whose sad condition I did seriously bewail.

So powerful a narrative patently deserves a circulation wider than the readers of Miss Child's footnotes (who must be a very select group, if not actually extinct). The 'diary of Anthony Abbott', as it purports to be, parallels and complements the well known *Declaration* by John Ivie (the mayor to whom Abbott refers), which describes the same calamitous visitation of plague on Salisbury in 1627.

The style is somewhat flowery and suspiciously more literary than is commonly found in contemporary archives – but then it is a vivid personal record, not the 'righteous dullness' of an official report. But is it an authentic record written by a witness of the terrible events it describes, or was it concocted by a literary forger, Salisbury's Thomas Chatterton?

The text offers several facts for the historian to pursue in the quest for authentication. Who was Anthony Abbott? The family name is not uncommon in contemporary archives of Salisbury. James Abbott was elected mayor in November 1627. No mention of Anthony though has come to light. He was not a member of the corporation, nor did he leave a will to be proved in the local courts, and no mention of him has come to light in contemporary archives. The burial of his wife whose death he relates in June 1627 is not recorded in the registers of the city parishes of St Edmund or St Thomas or of the Cathedral. The registers of St Martin's have not survived for the second quarter of the 17th century and frustratingly the copies required to be sent annually to the bishop begin in July 1627. Such a lacuna could be the result of the hiatus caused by the plague, which might also have led to omissions in the extant registers. No other persons are mentioned by name although the mayor is presumably John Ivie, the self-acclaimed civic hero of the plague whose own memoir (his *Declaration*, referred to above) was published in 1661.[1]

Internal evidence is not sufficiently conclusive to establish authenticity beyond the historian's criteria of reasonable doubt. Where does this leave the quest? A clue may lie in the source of the text, described in the header of the page on which it begins (359) as 'Gleanings from the Muniment Room'. Since there is no apparent link with the episcopal, chapter or diocesan records (then kept in the cathedral muniment room), the strongest candidate by far must be the Salisbury city archives. These in Miss Child's day resided in what was then known as Salisbury's Council House (now the guildhall), but have been held, since 1980, in the Wiltshire (now Wiltshire & Swindon) Record Office in Trowbridge. Perusal of the catalogue of these municipal archives draws a blank, which is not surprising in the light of the extensive mining of the 17th-century material by Professor Paul Slack, who makes no reference to it.[2]

The archives include however a detailed manuscript descriptive list completed by 1910 by T H Baker, the distinguished antiquarian and farmer from Mere, whose considerable body of transcriptions of parish registers and monumental inscriptions from South Wiltshire is well known. Baker worked methodically through the containers and packages of archives to produce a detailed inventory.[3] Pages 58-73 of the list describe the contents of a portfolio which largely comprised papers about musters and trained bands from the late 16th century to 1637. There were also several documents relating to the plague in the city between 1625 and 1627. One records the appointment of three searchers, presumably charged with the task of seeking out victims and enforcing quarantine, two of whom were women. This tallies with the text, our first corroborative evidence, but no more than a crumb. Page 62 contains the briefest of mentions of a letter about the plague, 1627. Could this be Abbott's account? Baker, finding a single item, might have described it thus; Miss Child may have assumed that it was an extract of something more substantial and that such a chronological account could only be a diary.

Sadly the contents of the portfolio appear to have been lost by 1949 when the distinguished archivist Dr Albert Hollaender imposed an arrangement of the muniments that is retained to the present day. The chances of the documents reappearing might be slim, although encouragement may be drawn from the fate of the city charter of 1285, which was removed between 1950 and 1980, only to resurface in 2001.

And if we turn our attention from the unsolved problem of Anthony Abbott's lost diary to the question of Miss Child, transcriber or forger, the picture does not become much clearer. To take a leaf out of her book, 'So just who was this Spinster verbose | Who made her home in Sarum's fair Close?'

Three census returns record Miss Child's residence in the Close.[4] The first (1841) is brief, revealing that she was aged about 40, of independent means and not born in Wiltshire. In 1861 much the same information is given, her age being 67 and birthplace Romsey, Hants. The intervening census is more informative giving her occupation as 'Fundholder & Author in Subjects of Topography'. Unusually no live-in servant is shown in any of the census returns, perhaps due to the size of the house which she herself describes in her poem as 'a tiny abode, well befitting a spinster'.

She lived alone, without pets but with many books to occupy her as well as sewing and housework. Her house, number 52 (now the offices of the Friends of the Cathedral), situated on the corner of the north side of Choristers' Green, is well placed to see all the comings and goings of both normal daily activity and special events like the installation of a new Bishop. On such days she was always 'at home' to her friends, offering hospitality in the form of 'A *tiny* decanter, a *wee* cake on a tray'.

She produced a number of other poems on Salisbury events such as the Exhibition at the Council Chamber in 1852 and the Peace Celebrations of 1856, but her chief claim to fame as an author is *The Spinster at Home*. Published on 14 December 1844, with three illustrations, price 10 shillings, available in Salisbury and London, it was presumably aimed at the Christmas trade. This is confirmed by a comment in the following week's *Salisbury Journal* that many would consider it 'as an interesting gift for the approaching season'[5]

She must have accumulated a sizeable collection of notes while working in *The Spinster at Home* which could perhaps have shed more light on her sources, but their fate is unknown. In her will, made a few months before her death, she leaves all her books to her cousin Edward Atkins, of Basset, Hants but no mention is made of notebooks or documents.[6]

Her death on the 28 November 1869 was marked by a brief notice in the *Salisbury Journal* and a short obituary in the *Salisbury Standard & Wilts Advertiser*.[7] This revealed that she was, at 83, the oldest inhabitant of the Close (a fact not entirely consistent with her age on the census returns!) but gave no details of her background. An entry in the Romsey parish register which records the baptism of Frances, daughter of Mr Jos'h Child & Frances his wife on 15 January 1787, presumably refers to her. No description or picture of her has so far been found. She was buried on 2 December in the cloister garth at the Cathedral.

References

1 Reprinted in Slack, P.A. 1975, *Poverty in Early Stuart Salisbury*. Wiltshire Record Society (31), 109-34
2 Slack, *op. cit.*
3 WSRO G23/129/5.
4 1841 Census HO107/1190/8 folio 9; 1851 Census HO 107/1846 folio 499; 1861 Census RG 9/1315 folio 49. Information has been kindly supplied by Miss S Eward, Librarian and Keeper of the Muniments, Salisbury Cathedral
5 *Salisbury Journal* 14 & 21 Dec 1844,
6 Will proved 17 Dec 1869, Salisbury District Probate Registry, effects under £4000. £100 to the Cathedral Restoration Fund with various bequests to friends and family.
7 *Salisbury Journal & Salisbury Standard & Wilts Advertiser*, both 4 Dec 1869.

William Butterfield and the Restoration of the Church of St Mary, Dinton in 1875

Michael Drury

It should be said, at the outset, that there is nothing exceptional about William Butterfield's restoration of Dinton church. The building was in a poor state of repair and Butterfield's intervention was important for its continued well-being, but its dilapidated condition certainly did not make it exceptional. Our medieval parish churches had been taken for granted for far too long and by the nineteenth century had deteriorated fairly uniformly to a general state of disrepair. The restoration at Dinton church is of interest nonetheless for it typifies

William Kemm's north view of Dinton church in 1865, shortly before restoration.
(Reproduced by kind permission of Salisbury & South Wilts Museum)

those undertaken elsewhere. Its very ordinariness makes it a good indicator of the changing fortunes that befell our parish churches in the latter half of the nineteenth century. By looking at this one restoration in some detail, we may better understand the situation that pertained locally and perhaps more widely too.

Perhaps the single most significant aspect of the restoration of St Mary's, Dinton was the choice of architect. For although the most conspicuous architects of the Gothic Revival in South Wiltshire were members of the Wyatt family, it was William Butterfield, one of the most famous architects of his day and perhaps the architect most closely associated with High Victorian Gothic who won the commission at Dinton church in 1873.

The Gothic Revival in South Wiltshire started early. In 1789 James Wyatt imposed upon Salisbury Cathedral a view of Gothic as seen through the trained eyes of a fashionable architect of the time. But the trained eyes of the time were schooled in classical architecture and as such, although Wyatt appreciated the picturesque, he looked for order. He removed that which did not comply with the original thirteenth century conception and tidied up the rest with a neo-classical understanding of presentation. The greatest impact on the interior resulted largely from the installation of clear glass and the whitening of the wall surfaces. James Wyatt may have understood the form and spatial quality of the building but his work indicates little interest in antiquarian matters and he clearly had no appreciation of the complex layering of medieval gothic or of the importance of the ancient surfaces and the medieval materials themselves.

The other great example of the Gothic Revival in South Wiltshire at the end of the eighteenth century was the extraordinary and now almost vanished Fonthill Abbey, also by James Wyatt. But these commissions were still isolated instances against the predominantly neo-classical taste of the day. Although James Wyatt's nephew Jeffry was later knighted as Sir Jeffry Wyattville for his gothicising of Windsor Castle, Philipps House, his mansion of 1813-1816 for the Wyndhams near Dinton Church, is still firmly in the neo-classical tradition. It was not until Pugin, who built St Marie's Grange for himself in Alderbury in 1835 that the tide really began to change strongly in this part of the country, or indeed elsewhere. Pugin was the great Gothic publicist. His book *Contrasts* (first published in Salisbury in 1836) extolled the virtues of Gothic and compared it to the debased classical offerings that typified much of the new building going up at the time in Salisbury and elsewhere.

This resurgence of Gothic had a lot to do with the decaying condition of our parish churches and their need for repair. The new enthusiasm for the Gothic style turned repair into restoration, in an attempt to not only address the ravages of time but to put these now-venerated buildings back to their original appearance, however dimly this original conception was perceived. Isolated instances in the early 19th century had become a torrent by 1850. A survey of 55 churches in South East Wiltshire found that almost half were destroyed or drastically altered in the nineteenth century.[1] Of these, eight were completely demolished, five more almost completely, while many others were dismantled and parts re-integrated into new churches. Twenty-four were radically restored and extended and all were subject to restoration to at least some degree.

In the area around Dinton the earliest example was at Teffont Evias, an early picturesque Gothic composition, re-built by Charles Fowler in 1824-1826. The rectory was by Scott in 1842. The re-building of the spire at Chilmark had been undertaken much earlier in 1760 but this was presumably due to sheer necessity, as the re-building of the north side including the arcade did not follow until 1856. George Gilbert Scott was at work in nearby Swallowcliffe in 1842-3 too, where his somewhat cumbersome Romanesque style reflected a relatively short-lived national revival of that style in the early 1840s. By the time Wylye church was re-built in 1844-6 that moment had passed, but not before the movement had produced its finest offering, the spectacular new church at Wilton. Built between 1841 and 1845, it typified the best of the nation's fleeting preoccupation with the Romanesque.

The architect at Wilton was another Wyatt. Thomas Henry, more frequently known as T.H. Wyatt, was a distant cousin of Wyattville and one more generation further still from James Wyatt. His dates, 1807-80, overlap by only six years those of James Wyatt, who died in 1813. T.H. Wyatt was the most prolific architect of the Gothic Revival in south Wiltshire, and indeed in Wiltshire as a whole. Much of this sprang from the patronage of the influential Herbert family at Wilton, hence his commission for their grand church. Earlier he had built a chapel for them at Wilton House. T.H. Wyatt was also the consulting architect to the newly formed Salisbury Diocesan Church Building Association in 1836. He worked at the Bishop's Palace in Salisbury and built almost twenty new churches in the county including Fonthill Gifford, South Newton and Lower Bemerton, the latter for the Herbert family again. Indeed they were influential in his appointment elsewhere in the Wylye and Nadder valleys where he worked widely with major re-builds at Fovant and Sutton Mandeville in 1862 and 1863 and Little Langford in 1864. Alvediston, Bowerchalke and Burcombe were among thirty churches which he largely rebuilt elsewhere in the county. T.H. Wyatt restored as many more again, including Fonthill Bishop in south Wiltshire and others, too numerous to mention, further afield.

But Wyatt was not the only architect working in Wiltshire. Although the Herberts at Wilton remained faithful to T.H. Wyatt in the main, this was not always the case. They paid for his new churches at South Newton and Bemerton as well as Wilton and contributed to the cost of many of the other restorations that they commissioned from him, but they brought in someone else to work at Netherhampton church in 1876. This was William Butterfield.

Butterfield had been the chosen architect of a neighbouring great family, the Earls Nelson at Trafalgar House, on the Avon between Salisbury and Downton. Although T.H. Wyatt had earlier built the new church at Charlton All Saints for them, Butterfield built the school nearby in 1857 and restored the chapel at Standlynch, near Trafalgar House in 1859. He worked at Trafalgar House too in that year and later restored Whiteparish church for them in 1870 and re-built Landford church in 1858. Throughout Wiltshire, Butterfield worked in twenty five or more churches, including Amesbury, Heytesbury and St George's, Harnham, south of the plain. His work at St Mary's, Dinton between 1873 and 1876 was followed at nearby St Edith's, Baverstock in 1882.

So who was William Butterfield? Firstly, and perhaps most importantly, William Butterfield was the architect who built All Saints, Margaret Street, London. It has been argued that All Saints was the nineteenth century's most influential church.[2] With it, in 1848, High Victorian Gothic sprang into being. His work is characterised by structural polychromy, colour being integral to the structure rather than applied to its surface. Externally, bands and zig-zags of coloured brick break up the walls; internally, materials and patterns vary prodigiously, all precise and hard yet vibrant with colour: geometric roundels of tiles, polished granite piers, stripes and zig-zags of brick and tile proliferate.

Perhaps Butterfield's best known building is Keble College Chapel in Oxford, built to commemorate John Keble, poet-priest of the Tractarian movement that represented the High Church wing of the gothic revival. Keble died in 1866 and Butterfield completed not only the chapel but the whole college between 1868 and 1882 on the proceeds of an extraordinarily successful public appeal. But it is the chapel itself which is the *tour de force* and it was this commission that established Butterfield as the leading architect in the Tractarian movement nationally.

As a consequence, Butterfield was often the choice where the donors or sponsors of a restoration project had High Church leanings, as at Trafalgar House for the Earls Nelson. Sidney Herbert at Wilton was fully aware of the Tractarian movement too, being a friend from his Oxford days of John Henry (Cardinal) Newman, the most committed of them all and later a Catholic convert. After the death of John Keble, it was Newman who led the crusade to restore Catholic ideas of ritual and theology to the Anglican Church and it was presumably through such connections that William Butterfield's name was put forward for the work at Dinton church. In April 1873 he was requested by the Rev Cholmely, Vicar of Dinton to examine and report upon the condition of Dinton church, following a letter from Mrs Starky of Bromham who, as a member of the Wyndham family, used to live in Dinton. Mrs Starky had written to the vicar earlier that year:

I still retain a great love and affection for my old most happy home and for some years I have been anxious that the church should be properly repaired and put in good order … but I have delayed to mention my wish until I was in a position to assist materially … I sincerely hope you will not be indisposed to approve of my great wish and that you will assist in carrying it out. If so, and you will employ some competent person to make an estimate, I will then inform you how much I will contribute.[3]

Mrs Starky expressed her desire that a gallery at the west end of the church should be removed and that the new seats throughout the church should be of oak and open to all users. Butterfield visited and reported on the condition of the church:

The transepts are on the whole in the worst condition of any part of the church and parts of these, and the gable end at least of the north porch ought to be taken down and re-built – large general repairs of the walls and windows are necessary and some new roofs – all the roofs should be stripped of their tiles and re-tiled and all roofs repaired – the church is much buried in the ground, more especially on the north side of the nave. This makes the walls very damp and injures much of the dignity of the church – the belfry is in a disgraceful condition, the bells being very crowded and the framing out of condition – I do not know how far it is contemplated to put to rights such works as these. I think the church would well admit of an outlay of £1,500 but I have not made any minute estimate.[4]

Butterfield prepared preliminary drawings and when Mrs Starky saw his report she at once promised to give £500 at least. Accordingly a notice was fixed to the church door and a public meeting was called. The meeting was well attended and the vestry book[5] records that the following resolutions were all unanimously carried:

1. Resolved that this meeting is agreed that the parish church of Dinton is in a condition which is very unbecoming for a place dedicated to the worship and service of Almighty God, that it requires much repair and restoration and to be reseated throughout.
2. Resolved that this meeting desires to return its most hearty thanks to Mrs Starky for her voluntary and most generous offer of £500 and this meeting promises to use every effort to raise whatever further funds may be required.
3. The ratepayers of Dinton understanding that the church has been examined by Mr Butterfield, a skilled architect, who estimates the total cost of properly repairing and reseating the church in oak at not less than £1,600, understanding also that the sum of £150 at the least is required for the building of a school in addition to all sums which have been actually promised or may reasonably be counted on from other sources, do agree to raise by way of a loan upon the security of the rates a sum of £650 and that application be made to the

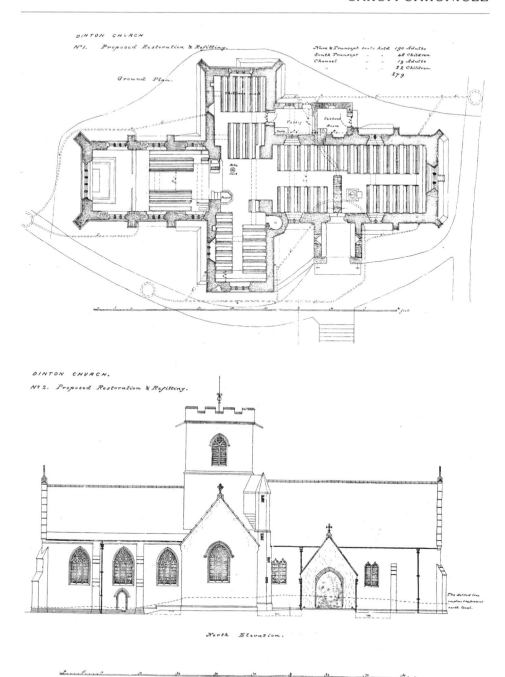

Butterfield's plan and north elevation for the proposed restoration and refitting. The elevation includes his proposal for reducing the churchyard ground levels on the north side where they were causing dampness in the church. The old level is indicated by the dotted line on the north elevation.

landowners of the parish for such consent and co-operation on their part as may be necessary to give security for the loan.

4. Resolved that this meeting agrees that Mr Butterfield be requested to be the architect for all the work to be done in and upon the church and for the building of the new school and teacher's house.

Mr Wyndham of Philipps House, the adjoining landowner, did not consent to the plan for raising money by way of a loan on the security of the parish rates so this resolution was not acted upon, but it was nonetheless resolved to obtain the plans and specifications in accordance with the other resolutions. When these were ready a letter was circulated in the parish and another meeting called to consider them. This meeting was held in the schoolroom on Monday 12 January 1874 and was attended by Mr Wyndham and some 62 of the parishioners. The whole of the plans and drawings for the repair and re-seating of the church were exhibited one by one to the meeting and explanations given. Mr Wyndham asked some questions and made some objections to detail but finally the proposals were carried unanimously.

The faculty was granted on the 27 March 1874 and although the date of commencement on site is unknown, the works were completed by 1876. The condition of the church can be seen, prior to restoration, in watercolours dated 1804 and 1865 (?) by John Buckler[6] and R Kemm[7] respectively. Butterfield's restoration can best be assessed by a close inspection in conjunction with the architect's own specification which survives in the Wiltshire & Swindon Record Office.[8]

St Mary's, Dinton is a fine medieval church of mixed date, now predominantly in the early fourteenth-century Decorated style although the transepts are a little earlier. A crossing tower, the top of which is later and Perpendicular, dominates the un-aisled cruciform composition, as seen from the approaches from the village which stands further down the hill to the south and east. From these viewpoints the tower stands above the high chancel with its magnificent five-light east window, well proportioned and with splendidly dignified intersecting tracery. Elements of earlier work can be seen in the Norman or Transitional font and in the north door, where carved work of about 1200 survives in the capitals.

The church is built on ground rising to the north and here Butterfield found the levels of the churchyard to have built up, as was commonly the case in ancient churchyards. To reduce dampness he specified lowering the levels externally while the earth within the church was to be removed to a depth of 12 inches beneath the joists of the wooden floors. All vaults for which permission could be obtained were to be filled in and other vaults and graves were to be adapted to suit the new levels. Externally all the plinths were to be repaired after the earth had been lowered, all weeds removed from the masonry and the masonry pointed and repaired. Walls and buttresses were to be shored up and underpinned and repaired where necessary after the lowering of the earth. In conjunction with this, the north wall of the porch was to be taken down and re-built, the existing jamb and arch stones being re-used, where sound.

The remainder of the masonry restoration externally is mostly associated with the raising of the gable parapets to accommodate Butterfield's new roofs and, although there is much new work in the south wall of the south transept, his condemnation of the condition of the transepts in his earlier report might have suggested a more significant intervention. The rebuilding of the north wall of the porch however is uncompromising. Sharply cut from durable local stone, it remains characteristically indicative of Butterfield's repair philosophy. Clearly, new work should be seen as such, with no attempt to soften its impact against the patina of the ancient masonry adjacent.

The amount of masonry replacement generally is remarkably small for such a major restoration at this time. Although the sandy limestone of Tisbury and Chilmark is durable as walling stone or ashlar it does not fare so well as window dressings, yet only the gable window of the south transept appears in Butterfield's specification for replacement. Butterfield had all the plain glass in the church re-leaded, saving what old glass he could and making up with new best Newcastle crown glass. He specifically excluded stained glass, beautiful medieval fragments of which survive in the north and south facing windows of the sanctuary. The reason for this minimal schedule of work to the masonry of the windows is that earlier restoration work had preceded Butterfield's campaign. Between 1840 and 1850 a more or less continuous programme of repair was undertaken. This phase of work is described in the back of a register of christenings[9] and elsewhere[10] among the parish records. It is an incomplete record but contains specific references to 'mullions in the chancel', 'tracery of the west window', 'one window to the north and the east window entirely re-glazed and the remaining tracery of all windows restored'. Butterfield's reference to the surviving fragments of stained glass is explained by an entry that reads: 'the stained glass from the chancel was, with a small addition, placed in the window to the south of the altar and in the head of the window to the north.'

Internally, all floors, pavements, steps, seats and fittings not forming part of the new plan were to be taken up and entirely removed from the church. The west gallery was taken down and removed. Wall monuments were to be preserved as were the inscription brasses which were to be re-laid in the new pavement. This new pavement was formed in red and black tile, new oak pews being placed on new joisted timber pew islands. The red and black tiles were supplied by Peake's while the chancel was paved with Minton's red, black and encaustic tiles.

Butterfield restored the fine Purbeck marble font, cleaning, repairing and re-fixing it on new stone steps, forming drainage beneath. He also specified a

Butterfield's rebuilt porch, showing the contrast between new and old work.

font cover. His uncompromising approach leaves the venerable old font to stand comparison with the hard edges of the new stone steps; but by so doing he showed it to best advantage, raising the font high enough to allow its carved sides to be appreciated.

The re-fitting of the church was a fundamentally important aspect of the restoration as far as the vicar and the church community were concerned. As with many other clients at the time, they found the old box pews and galleries quite unsuitable for contemporary worship. The provision of free seating was fundamental to the restoration movement, be it Tractarian or otherwise, and here as elsewhere it was free seating numbers that were used to argue the case for the removal of the earlier furnishings. Butterfield's new fittings are in his usual simple geometrical style, fairly austere but making no attempt at copying any medieval precedent. All were in Riga oak, with walnut capping to the altar rail and walnut intermixed in the new pulpit too. The altar table was in Riga wainscot with a walnut top. Most of the pews and all of the major elements of liturgical furnishing survive and still form a good set today.

Butterfield's work at Dinton church should be set within the national context of literally thousands of parish church restorations throughout the country in the nineteenth century. At Dinton, Butterfield's proposals were accepted practically without question. Elsewhere, for example in the parish of Christleton (Cheshire) he had rather more difficulty. There he advocated the incorporation of the old tower rather than a complete rebuilding, telling the parish meeting:

> Half the buildings in Europe owe their character and interest to their system of preserving what is sound in the older parts. . . Unless you want a much larger church than you would expect, then you had better keep the old tower and so look a little different to the modern new churches which are generally so noisy and pretentious.[11]

In the end Christleton accepted Butterfield's advice too but the episode is of interest on two counts. It shows that William Butterfield was mindful of the sequential development of our parish churches and it indicates his opinion of the average new Victorian church. If they are generally 'noisy and pretentious', then by inference he considered his own contributions relatively quiet and unpretentious. Later critics have not always considered this to be the case, his reputation (and that of Victorian architecture generally) reaching a low point in the 1950s. As late as 1974 that well known lover of the English parish church, Alec Clifton Taylor, accused Butterfield of having no regard for the *genius loci* and the Victorians generally of being insensitive to materials. How otherwise can be explained, he asks 'their addiction to hard shiny surfaces in juxtaposition with old stonework. . . Their excursions into polychromy are usually embarrassing because of the stridency of the colours used'.[12] In the same year

The church from the south in 1984 before Butterfield's chimney was taken down. The vestry roof still has a polycarbonate covering today in place of his tiles.

The church from the south-east.

H S Goodhart-Rendel, chairman of the Victorian Society, suggested that 'Defiant is the word that fits the usual temper of this coarse-grained genius', writing of encaustic tiling on the east wall of the sanctuary at Amesbury, 'now mercifully hidden by curtains'.[13] His opinion is still shared by some today and indeed at Amesbury the hanging that conceals the tiles in question has recently been renewed. Happily Butterfield's reputation, and those of the other great Victorian architects, is now assured and similar hangings at Dinton and Baverstock have been removed.

Dinton can consider itself fortunate. William Butterfield's restoration was conservative and sensitive for its time. Completed in 1876, it measures up well against the manifesto of William Morris's Society for the Protection of Ancient Buildings, written in 1877 as a result of the widespread and insensitive interventions into the ancient fabric of our historic churches elsewhere. Internally Butterfield's work is obvious, due to the uniformity of his re-furnishing, but there can be no doubt that the re-seating of the church was fundamentally important to the parish and it is unfair to blame Butterfield entirely for the removal of all the earlier fittings. He was, after all, caught up in a national debate that is clearly reflected in a letter written to a local paper by 'An Octogenarian Pew Renter'.[14] No-one questions, says the writer 'the laudable desire to increase the accommodation of a church for the labouring classes' and 'no-one in these days is disposed to support the old practice of devoting large spaces in the church to the unnecessary indulgence or caprice of powerful individuals'. The reason for re-seating churches in the late nineteenth century was clearly laudable in social terms and we can hardly blame Butterfield for his typically uncompromising approach to his client's pragmatic requirement for undiscriminatingly uniform seating.

Today the church guidebook[15] implores the reader to try and keep the village centre unspoiled. It is typical, it says, of all that is best in the English countryside. The village may not have fared too well in terms of new developments elsewhere in recent years but thanks to all involved in its 1875 restoration, the church at least still stands almost as it did at the end of the middle ages, largely unspoiled.

Notes

1 Royal Commission on the Historic Monuments of England, *Churches of South-East Wiltshire*, 1987, p.70.
2 Chris Brooks, *The Gothic Revival*, 1999, p.309.
3 Unpublished letter from Charlotte Starky in Bromham, Chippenham, 24 February 1873, Dinton Church Restoration Notes, 1875, Vestry Book, Wiltshire & Swindon Record Office (WSRO), Trowbridge.
4 Unpublished extracts from a report by William Butterfield on Dinton Church, Dinton Church Restoration Notes,

1875, Vestry Book, Dinton Parish Papers, WSRO, Trowbridge.

5 Dinton Church Restoration Notes, 1875, Vestry Book, Dinton Parish Papers, WSRO, Trowbridge.

6 Buckler Watercolours, 1804, ii12, Wiltshire Archaeological & Natural History Society Library, Devizes.

7 R.Kemm Drawings, 1/40, Salisbury Museum.

8 Specification and drawings by William Butterfield, Dinton Parish Papers, WSRO, Trowbridge.

9 Notes on a blank page in the Register of Christenings, Dinton Parish Papers, WSRO, Trowbridge.

10 Undated letter to the Archdeacon, author unknown, concerning 1840s repairs, Dinton Parish Papers, WSRO, Trowbridge.

11 Paul Thompson, *William Butterfield*, 1971, p.48.

12 Alec Clifton Taylor, *English Parish Churches as Works of Art*, 1974, pp.11-12.

13 *Ibid*, p.12.

14 *Salisbury and Winchester Journal*, 6 May 1876, p.7.

15 Anon., *Dinton Church Guide*, undated, pp.7-8.

Salisbury as a Seaport: some further debate

Michael Cowan

I am grateful that you have published the excellent article by Don Cross on the 17th-century Avon Navigation,[1] building on his 1972 work and providing a new and definitive base line for the topic. It is of great help to my own current research on the floated water meadows between Britford and Downton. Most were created at about the same time as the Navigation and that part of the valley must have been quite crowded with water engineers!

Can I add to the debate on the evidence that trading craft did reach Salisbury from the sea? The affidavits (quoted by both Nancy Steele in 1982 and in the recent article in *Sarum Chronicle*[2]) indicate thirty to forty year old first hand memories of, in effect, regular traffic: probably good evidence but not contemporary. Hugh Shortt seems to create the modern understanding by categorically stating that 'by 1684 two vessels laden with twenty five tons could be brought up to Crane Bridge'.[3] He gives no reference but repeats the assertion, and some phrasing, from Henry Hatcher's work of 1843.[4] Hatcher was writing some century and a half after the event, but fortunately cites his source: Ledger D folio 270 of Salisbury Chronicle H' from Salisbury City records [which are now in WSRO]. Several versions survive among the city records of lists of mayors and notable events,[5] and it may be such a list to which Hatcher refers. No extant list, however, includes this information.

Is the wherry shown sailing upstream in *Landscape with a view of Salisbury Cathedral* illustrating Don Cross's article based on observation, or oral tradition – or just artistic licence to enhance the composition? The picture is provenanced in New South Wales as 'J Browne … oil on canvas … eighteenth century'. A more precise date would help. Grove's *Dictionary of Artists* has a very short piece on J Browne 1741 – 1801, described as a specialist engraver. It records that he produced etchings of four of his own 'drawings' of a landscape nature published in the late 1790s. If this is the right artist then the presence of the sailing craft is based on very distant oral evidence, or no evidence at all. Hatcher also (page 460) refers to a work in relation to the proposed Navigation by Francis Matthew in 1665 describing 'small flat bottomed vessels, bilanders of

30 tons drawing three of water'. Bilander, from a Dutch root, is defined in a modern dictionary as 'a small two masted vessel for coasting or for river or coastal navigation'. They sound on the big side, and I wonder if the reference informs or just confuses the debate.

My second point concerns motive power. Oars are unlikely; manpower is costly and eats into cargo space. That leaves haulage by men or horses, sailing, or poling. Or probably a mix of some or all of these methods. There is little doubt that craft can be sailed in the most unlikely waters. There is an interesting illustration of vessels on the Thames in a recent publication.[6] A rather rectangular barge with a mast but no sail hoisted is being drawn upstream by six horses in line. Coming downstream is a somewhat similar craft under sail – and apparently on a collision course.

Cross in 1972 and 2003 suggests poling and sailing, and implicitly discounts haulage, except presumably through any flash locks, pointing out correctly that there is no evidence of a tow path. A century later, on the plans for Salisbury's other failed canal to Kimbridge, there was to be 'a tow-path 9 ft wide; a gravel path only 2 ft wide along it suggests that the towing was expected to be done by men'.[7] There is nothing similar for the earlier Avon Navigation *except* for a map quoted nowhere, to my knowledge, other than by Nancy Steel in 'Sir Joseph Ashe, Bt, 1617 – 1686 an advocate of watermeadows in good husbandry'.[8] In this, referring to major water meadow works, she records that

Pound Lock at Britford on the Salisbury Avon navigation, photographed by the author in June 2004 (copyright Michael Cowan)

In 1686 a 'View' was made to examine the number and size of drains and cuts along the west side of the river bank over which navigation bridges would have to be made 'sufficient for men and horses to pass over' to haul barges. Seventy seven bridges had to be built … The smallest bridges were over 3 – 4 foot drains, the longest was 35 feet over the Main Cut. In the 1712 map of new Court Farm, the bridges … are marked.

Seventy seven bridges, even simple plank ones, is an awful lot of work, and cost some £190 for the benefit of the Navigation paid out of a total of perhaps £2,000 by the Sir Joseph Ashe in developing his own water meadows. This at least suggests that haulage was a serious intent, and the map itself might help to determine the matter rather better. Nancy Steele cites 'Longford Castle MSS' for it. Much Longford material has since gone to WSRO but (at the time of writing) neither end can find it!

Finally, may I endorse the plea that the pound lock at Britford is worthy of formal protection? It is thoroughly recorded in Cross 1972, and the illustration shows it in a sorry state in June 2004. There are innumerable pound locks surviving from the later eighteenth century onwards but there can only be a very few from the seventeenth. This industrial archaeology rarity is not scheduled or listed, nor is it on Wiltshire County Council's Sites and Monuments Record. Who will take up that particular cudgel?

References

1 *Sarum Chronicle* 3, 35-44
2 WSRO 490/1683
3 *City of Salisbury* 1957, 81
4 *Old and New Sarum*, 480
5 WSRO G23/1/235
6 Simon Thurley, *Hampton Court* 2003, endpapers and page 237
7 Hugh Braun 'The Salisbury Canal – a Georgian misadventure *WANHM* 58 1962, 171-80
8 *Hatcher Review* 2 (13) 1982, 125-32

The Great Deception:
Mathematical Tiles in Salisbury

Richard Durman

S alisbury's place in architectural history is permanently assured by the
presence of its cathedral and of the houses of the Close. Yet there are also
aspects of building practice in Salisbury that deserve more than a
footnote. One is the widespread use of stone from Ham Hill in Somerset
resulting in the largest collection of Hamstone buildings outside its local region.[1]
Another is the unusually extensive usage (mainly in the Georgian era) of
'mathematical tiles', a form of wall cladding that is something of a Salisbury
speciality. Only three other towns in England (Brighton, Lewes and Canterbury)
have more of them and they are unknown outside England and Wales.

The development and use of mathematical tiles has long been of interest
to architectural historians and industrial archaeologists as well as to architects
and building practitioners. In 1981 the topic was graced by a national
symposium held at Ewell in Surrey under the chairmanship of Alec Clifton-
Taylor. A paper on mathematical tiles in Wiltshire was read by Nicholas Moore,
then working in Salisbury as an RCHME[2] investigator. Soon afterwards the
Wiltshire Building Record (WBR) set up its own register of relevant buildings in
Wiltshire in conjunction with the Weald and Downland Open Air Museum in
Singleton, West Sussex. The most important work in relation to Salisbury has
been undertaken by Salisbury architect, Gerald Steer, who drafted a paper in
1986 (since revised and updated) containing an architectural analysis of the use
of the tiles in Salisbury and identifying a number of other sites where he has
discovered that they had been used. The paper has not yet been formally
published but he has supplied copies to interested parties including WBR.[3]

Mathematical tiles share some of the characteristics of the more common
overlapping 'hanging tiles' (made to clad the vertical face of a building) but are
different in that they are *intended to appear as brickwork*. In other words they
represent a deceit on the part of the original owner or builder. And, in many
cases, no ordinary deceit, because mathematical tiles were often made to look
like the most expensive form of brick, namely 'rubbed' or 'gauged' brick. This
style of brick was fashionable in Georgian times, mainly for use in lintels or

arches above the doorways and windows of houses, but occasionally for an entire façade. It was an indication of quality, since the making of a single brick required a great deal of careful rubbing with abrasives so that it would fit as closely as possible to its neighbours. The ensuing hairline joint would be filled, not with ordinary mortar, but with lime putty, either 'neat' or mixed with a small amount of crushed stone. There are some good examples of rubbed brickwork above doors and windows in Salisbury (in Endless Street and St Ann's Street for example) but the only *apparent* examples of a façade of rubbed bricks (such as 64 High Street) are all in fact made of mathematical tiles. At any rate, this was true of the red tiles favoured throughout the earlier Georgian period. By the Regency period it became the vogue to use white bricks to match the chaste Grecian style then in fashion. 'White' bricks were actually grey or creamy-grey, the shade of many buildings of that period in Salisbury, and thus it is no surprise that the mathematical tiles of that time were also 'white' – and without any attempt to make them appear as rubbed bricks.

This false impression of brickwork is achieved by the *shape* of the tiles. Like ordinary hanging tiles, each mathematical tile leans out slightly from the plane of the wall in order to cover up part of the tile below. But what distinguishes it from the hanging tile is that its lower section has a vertical face and protrudes from the upper part of the tile. It is this lower section (and only this lower section) that will be on view, masquerading as a brick. If the deception

64 High Street – an example of false rubbed brickwork in mathematical tiles; the corner join (foreground) is covered by a piece of wood and a down pipe

is to succeed, great care needs to be taken in the accurate placement of each tile so that the brick-like portion lies as closely as possible to all its neighbours. It is this need for precision – both in manufacture and use – that may have given rise to the term 'mathematical tile'. The first recorded use of the term was by Sir John Soane in 1799 in reference to the price of such tiles.[4] Some of the other names by which they have been known are 'brick tiles' (the name that was, perhaps, most commonly used in the eighteenth century), 'weather tiles', 'geometric tiles' and 'mechanical tiles'.

A typical mathematical tile

The procedure for fixing them is much the same as hanging tiles: that is to say, the bottom row is fixed first so that the next row will overlap it and hide the upper section – and so on, until the top row is reached where some other way needs to be found of covering the top of the tile, such as a Classical cornice or (more mundanely) the barge boards to which the guttering is attached. The *way* they are fixed can vary. A common system in Salisbury was to nail them to timber boards (as is the standard practice in Hastings)[5] or to existing brickwork (as at 47 Winchester Street), but many were held in place by simply using plenty of rich lime mortar (as was done in Lewes)[6] with, perhaps, the use of nails on every so many tiles or rows. They were usually supplied with fixing holes – between one and four depending on the width of the tile. And the widths varied considerably to allow for the full range of bonds to be replicated.[7] Part of the deception was to ensure that the joints were pointed like real brickwork. But this was an awkward process – especially for the finer tiles – and in several cases in Salisbury it has not been carried out.

However well mathematical tiles have been fixed (and the joints pointed) there are sometimes ways in which their presence may be detected. The first is when one or more tiles become damaged or displaced and it becomes apparent that the tile is just that, and not the brick that it is pretending to be. There is an example of this at Windover House, St Ann's Street (Messrs Fawcetts) where the bottom few rows of tiles have been pushed out from the surface of the wall. The other principal 'give-away' is the treatment of the corners of the building or around the doors and windows. It was sometimes possible to obtain specially shaped tiles that would fit the corner of a building and maintain the illusion of continuous brickwork – particularly valuable where the sides of the building were being tiled as well as the front face. Examples of this may be seen at 31 Milford Street (part of the *Retreat Inn*) and at the *Cloisters* pub at the junction of Catherine Street and Ivy Street. But this was a difficult and

22-26 St Ann's Street after the front of the building had been re-hung with mathematical tiles (but before the ends were mortared) revealing the shape of the tiles

Part of The Retreat, Milford Street – the special corner tiles enhance the impression of brickwork, but the lowest row of tiles still gives the game away

expensive system and it was more common to cover the ends of the tiles by inserting a length of timber or some form of flashing. Examples of this method may be seen in the High Street near the Close Gate and in Catherine Street. And sometimes there has been little attempt to hide the ends – as at the Queen Street entrance to the Cross Keys Chequer or 59 Milford Street. The most difficult examples to detect (like 27 Catherine Street) are those that have been covered over in paint.

According to Clifton-Taylor, *hanging* tiles appeared in south-east England towards the end of the seventeenth century but 'brick-tiles were an invention of the Georgian period'.[8] Their earliest use in Salisbury may have been at 11 The Close (now Bishop Wordsworth's School), when the principal part of the house (fronting North Walk) was rebuilt 'probably in the 1750s'.[9] The front façade is in red brick with stone dressings but its side walls were hung with mathematical tiles, since replaced in part with ordinary hanging tiles. The heyday of the mathematical tile was between c1780 and c1840, and this corresponds with the ages of the bulk of the buildings in Salisbury where they have been used. One relatively late usage, and unusual for being outside the chequers or the Close, may be found at Milford Hill Cottage (near The Godolphin School). The creamy-yellow tiles that extend over most of three sides were probably added in the late nineteenth or early twentieth century when the building (of a few decades earlier) was altered. Here the tiles contrast with the grey brick of the original parts of the house. But at a nearby Victorian villa (45 Manor Road) the deep red tiles used for a narrow two-storey extension so closely match the existing brickwork that they are difficult to detect – though the lack of corner tiles gives the game away on closer inspection.

The reasons for the development of the mathematical tile were probably partly practical and partly aesthetic. By the last decades of the seventeenth century, brick had become established as the standard building material. Also, the Classical style, with its emphasis on symmetry and correct proportions, had become the architectural norm. It is interesting to compare, for example, the rather primitive brickwork and 'vernacular' style of Salisbury's earliest brick house (Cradock House, The Friary of 1616) with the more refined brickwork of, say, 9 and 19 The Close built about 50 years later. By Georgian times, the well-proportioned Classical façade was 'in' and the older vernacular styles were definitely 'out'. But it was expensive to demolish and rebuild one's house, so many owners of timber-framed buildings disguised them by covering them in brick or, more often, in mathematical tiles, which were light, took up less space (an important consideration where the building was flush with the street) and provided a weatherproof skin. A good example is the older portion of Watson's china shop in Queen Street. Its fascia bears the date '1306'. This is consistent with the timber-frame features seen inside the building but, on first inspection from the street, appears highly implausible on account of its Georgian-style brick façade. This was indeed an eighteenth-century addition, but the 'brick' actually consists of mathematical tiles. The timber building being tiled had often been built with one or more 'jetties' or overhangs. In some cases these have been obliterated by a new flat front (as at 82/84 Crane

William Russel's House (1306) with a fashionable Georgian makeover

Street); but at 36/38 St Ann's Street the jetty was retained – another clue that all is not as it seems.

Mathematical tiles could even be used to cover older 'unfashionable' brickwork. The leading example in Salisbury is 47 Winchester Street whose 'Georgianised', tiled south front contrasts oddly with the genuine seventeenth-century brickwork on its side walls. As mathematical tiles came to be more widely used they became a feature of new buildings from the outset. This is probably true of most of the Catherine Street examples. In such cases the use of tiles on a timber frame may simply have been a cheaper alternative to using brick as a load-bearing material but the tiles were expensive to buy and tricky to fix and this economic argument is by no means proven.[10]

It is often suggested that the tiles were the product of the brick tax: that the production of ordinary bricks was liable to the tax but that of tiles was not. Both Clifton-Taylor and Brunskill made this assumption in their leading works[11] and it is made plausible by the fact that the period of greatest popularity of the tiles (roughly 1780-1840) seems to coincide with the period during which the relevant Acts of Parliament were in force (1784-1850). However, in a paper delivered at the Ewell Symposium, Norman Nail came to the forthright conclusion that 'whatever is or is not clear about the history of brick tiles [as he preferred to call them] it is absolutely certain that their invention and use has no connection whatsoever with these taxes'. His paper demonstrated: (a) that tiles (including mathematical tiles) were taxed at rates that made their use no more advantageous than that of bricks; (b) that their use went back (he believed) perhaps as much as 100 years before the Act of 1784 and went on beyond its repeal; (c) that the tiles were always expensive to buy (because of the care which their manufacture demanded) and the taxation element would not have been a serious financial consideration; and (d) that although the tax on tiles was removed in 1834 there is no evidence of increased usage between then and 1850 when the tax on bricks was finally repealed. Another compelling reason why tax is unlikely to have affected the issue is the fact that the tiles were used in significant amounts only in certain areas of the country. Surely if this had been an efficient way of evading tax it would have been more widely used.

So where *are* mathematical tiles most likely to be found? In broad terms the answer is the south-east of England . . . and Salisbury! According to a list of known buildings in 1983,[12] the highest usage of mathematical tiles occurs in Sussex (382) and Kent (267), followed by Surrey (41), Hampshire and the Isle of Wight (37) and Wiltshire (33). The known tally for Wiltshire has since risen to 58, with all but five of them[13] in Salisbury. There is a scattering in other parts of England and Wales but no more than about 45 in total. The Appendix contains a list of Salisbury buildings identified either by WBR (in conjunction with the Open Air Museum) or by Gerald Steer. It should not be regarded as a complete or definitive list; Steer, for example, has identified another ten or so since his own list was first compiled. One surprisingly late addition to the list is Salisbury Guildhall, where black glazed tiles were used, presumably when it was first built, in the two blind windows at the eastern end of the building. That such a prominent building had previously been overlooked may be because the tiles are like no others in Salisbury (though they are common in Brighton) and one would not expect to find them in this location or used in this manner. Their presence has been given away by the fact that one or two are broken and it is possible to see that there is a space between the tile and the wall behind.

Why then should Salisbury come to have so many buildings containing mathematical tiles? Part of the explanation may lie in a particular combination of circumstances that applied to the city in the eighteenth century. Although it had lost the status it had enjoyed in the late middle ages, it remained a prosperous and fashionable place. On the other hand the large stock of timber-framed buildings it had inherited were no longer fashionable. Some had been rebuilt in brick, but many remained. In many instances, their owners would have felt that they were too well built to demolish and sought a face-lift for them instead; the mathematical tile was an ideal weapon in the battle for modernity. Another explanation may be that many of the older buildings in the chequers

Contrasting styles of wall cladding on medieval frontages in Minster Street: traditional hanging tiles on the right but mathematical tiles on the left

had been built hard up against the street and, although the erection of a new false façade of brickwork would have been too great an encroachment, a thin skin of tiles would not be noticed. Yet neither of these considerations accounts for their presence on many of the houses in the Close; nor for the 'new-build' examples (as in Catherine Street); nor for their use in the Victorian suburbs (Milford Hill Cottage and 45 Manor Road). So it may simply be that once they began to appear the idea caught on.

By its very nature good mathematical tiling is hard to detect, especially if painted. Repairs and alterations often reveal the secret. If you have come across examples not in the list of known buildings please send details to *Sarum Chronicle*. By keeping your eyes open when work is taking place you may be able to add to our knowledge of this form of construction.

Appendix of Buildings in Salisbury Known to Contain Mathematical Tiles (as at April 2004)

Butcher Row – 33.
Catherine Street – 12/14, 13, 17/19, 26/28, 27, 30, 38, 50 and Cloisters PH.
The Close – 11, 20, 26, 30, 31, 33.
Crane Street – 82/84.
Exeter Street – 108.
The Friary – extension to Windover House (see St Ann's Street).
High Street – 56/58, 59 and 64.
Manor Road – 45.
Market Place – The Guildhall.
Milford Hill – Milford Hill Cottage.
Milford Street – nos.13, 31 and 59
Minster Street – 11 and 15.
Oatmeal Row – no 15.
Queen Street – entrance to Cross Keys Chequer and 4 and 9.
St Ann's Street – 4, 6, 22-26 (Windover House) and 36/38.
St Nicholas Road – De Vaux Lodge.

St Thomas's Square – 2 and 28A Market Place
Silver Street – 37,38,40, 57, 58 and 59.
Winchester Street – 47.

[In addition, Gerald Steer knows of five other sites, not visible from the road, where a small area of tiling has taken place at some time.]

Four further examples of mathematical tiles which no longer exist were identified in RCHME *Salisbury I*, 1980:
13-13a New Canal (monument 186), north front rebuilt c1970
7-11 New Canal (187) demolished 1962
40 Catherine Street (195) demolished c1970
Toone's Court, Scot's Lane (383) demolished 'recently'.

Notes

1 See 'Hamstone in Salisbury', *Sarum Chronicle* 1 (2001) 29-36.
2 Royal Commission on Historical Monuments (England). Volume 1 of its report on Salisbury was published in 1980.
3 Gerald Steer. 'Mathematical Tiles in Salisbury'. [unpublished paper (first drafted 1986) deposited with the Wiltshire Building Record, Trowbridge. It is hoped that a version of this paper will be published in *Wiltshire Archaeological & Natural History Magazine* 98, 2005.
4 R.W. Brunskill. 1997. *Brick buildings in Britain*, 65
5 *Mathematical Tiles*, Notes of Ewell Symposium of 14 November 1981 [copy kindly supplied by Weald and Downland Open Air Museum, Singleton], 42.
6 Ibid.

7 Steer has identified tiles in Salisbury laid in the following bonds: Header, Stretcher, Flemish and Flemish Gardenwall.
8 A. Clifton-Taylor. 1972. *The Pattern of English Building*. London: Faber & Faber, 281.
9 RCHME, *The Houses of the Close*, 1993. London: Stationery Office, 86.
10 As was clear from the Ewell Symposium.
11 Clifton-Taylor 282; R.W. Brunskill. 1971. *Illustrated Handbook of Vernacular Architecture*. London: Faber & Faber, 61.
12 Contained in Issue 3 of the Ewell Symposium Notes.
13 The others are at Downton (1); Burbage (1); Marlborough (3): 'Known Examples of Mathematical Tiles in Wiltshire' (undated). List prepared by Wiltshire Building Record, Trowbridge.

The 150th Anniversary of the Charge of the Light Brigade

Peter Blacklock

In the *Salisbury and Winchester Journal* on 2 December 1854 the following announcement appeared:

> On the 6th (November) at Scutari, two days after the amputation of his leg, in consequence of wounds received at the battle of Balaclava, A F C Webb, Captain in the 17th Lancers, aged 22, youngest son of the late Frederick Webb, esq of Westwick, Durham, and Hamptworth, Hants, sincerely beloved and lamented by all who knew him.[1]

Augustus Webb had joined the regiment as a cornet at the age of 16, rising to lieutenant in 1850 and captain in 1852, so was with the 17th Lancers on that ill-fated day. The Charge of the Light Brigade at Balaclava on 25 October 1854 was the most notorious incident of the Crimean War reflecting both the superb gallantry of the soldiers and the incompetence of their commanding officers. Of nearly 700 who charged into the 'Valley of Death' to face the Russian artillery, only 195 returned. A French officer, watching the action, remarked: 'c'est magnifique, mais ce n'est pas la guerre'. The *Salisbury Journal*, too, was surprisingly critical, referring to 'deplorable results of misconceived instruction . . . fatal but heroic charge of the Light Brigade.'[2]

Captain Webb was hit and badly wounded in the leg, probably when the Russian guns were firing into the British cavalry at a range of only 80 yards. Three soldiers dragged him to safety under continuing fire. Sergeant John Farrel and Corporal John Berryman, both of the 17th Lancers, and Corporal Joseph Malone of the 13th Light Dragoons were each awarded the newly established Victoria Cross for their brave action.[3]

Casualties from the battle of Balaclava, including those of the Charge, were taken by sea to hospital in Scutari. The immediate cause of Captain Webb's death is not known, but as his leg had been amputated, he must have suffered enormous loss of blood, and the wound may have been gangrenous. He was buried at Scutari in grave number 31.

William Osmond, the noted Salisbury stonemason, carved a tablet with Gothic canopy which can now be seen on the west wall of the north transept of the cathedral. It reads:

SACRED

TO THE MEMORY

OF

FREDERICK WEBB ESQR.

OF WESTWICK, COUNTY OF DURHAM, AND

HAMPTWORTH IN THIS COUNTY.

YOUNGEST SON

OF THE LATE SIR JOHN WEBB, BARONET:

WHO DEPARTED THIS LIFE AT BRIGHTON

ON THE 4TH OF FEBRUARY 1846

AGED 56 YEARS.

ALSO OF HIS YOUNGEST SON

AUGUSTUS FREDERICK CAVENDISH WEBB ESQR.

CAPTAIN 17TH LANCERS

WHO DIED AT SCUTARI ON THE 6TH OF NOVR 1854

AGED 22 YEARS.

FROM WOUNDS RECEIVED IN THE BRILLIANT

LIGHT CAVALRY CHARGE AT BALAKLAVA

ON THE 25TH OF OCTOBER 1854.

The Webb family originally came to Salisbury from Cornwall via Shaftesbury. By 1500 they were one of the wealthiest and most influential families in the city, prospering as wool merchants and traders in other goods as far away as the Baltic Sea. Two Webbs were MPs, many were mayors, and John Webb in the 16th century became lord of the manor of Odstock. The family also owned the lordship of Hamptworth for some 200 years from the early 17th century. Members of the family, the Webbs of Odstock, played an important part in the continuation of the Roman Catholic faith in the area from the 16th to the 18th centuries. Sir John Webb, the fifth baronet, was Captain Webb's grandfather; his grandmother was Mary Ann Knight, who was the partner of Sir John after the death of his wife.[4]

One of the more macabre, but common sentimental traditions of the time was to return a lock of hair to the family of the deceased. Captain Webb's mother in England received this memento and wore it in a gold locket for the rest of her life. The locket formed part of a display in a major exhibition in summer 2004 at Belvoir Castle in Leicestershire to mark the anniversary of the Charge of the Light Brigade, along with many other military and personal memorabilia.[5]

Notes

1 *Salisbury and Winchester Journal*, 2 December 1854.

2 *Salisbury and Winchester Journal*, 18 November 1854. (Thanks to Ruth Newman for research into Salisbury Journals.)

3 Information from Terry Brighton, Assistant Curator, The Queen's Royal Lancers Regimental Museum, Grantham, Lincolnshire and from Mrs. Jean Perkins

4 Information from Raleigh St Lawrence (see The fortunes of a recusant family: the Webbs of Odstock, *The Hatcher Review*, Vol. 4, No. 39, Spring 1995.)

5 Information from Terry Brighton (as above).

The Hatcher Review was published biannually for twenty-five years, between 1976 and 2001, orginally from Salisbury and later from Winchester. Within its covers are to be found a bewildering range of papers, all concerned with 'Wessex history of more than local interest', as its masthead proclaimed. Hobnob Press has taken over the storage and distribution of those issues still available, and any proceeds from their sale, at £1 per issue (£2 issues 46-50) will help to finance future issues of *Sarum Chronicle*. Please write for details or visit the Hobnob Press website, www.hobnobpress.co.uk, where the issues still in print are listed.

Sarum Chronicle issues 1-3 are available from local booksellers, or from Hobnob Press, price £4.50 each.

Notes on Contributors

Peter Blacklock is a volunteer guide in Salisbury Cathedral and lives in the city.

John Chandler, formerly Wiltshire's local studies librarian, is a freelance historical researcher, writer, lecturer and editor, who has written and published (as Hobnob Press) widely about Wiltshire and regional history.

Lt Col (retd) Michael Cowan was Director at the former Great Barn Museum and has recently retired after thirteen years as Secretary of the British Association for Local History; he has long standing connections with many aspects of Wiltshire's local history

Michael Drury is an architect and author from Salisbury, specialising in historic building conservation.

Richard Durman is a retired local government lawyer/ administrator and is now a Salisbury City Guide with a special interest in buildings and architecture; his latest book, about Ham Hill Stone, is due to be published soon by Spire Books.

Steve Hobbs is an archivist at the Wiltshire & Swindon Record Office, whose edition of *Wiltshire Glebe Terriers* was published in 2003 by the Wiltshire Record Society.

Sue Johnson works part-time as library assistant at Wessex Archaeology, and is interested in local and family history. As a member of Salisbury Local History Group she contributed to *Caring*, its history of the city charities (1987).

Tim Tatton-Brown is a freelance archaeologist and architectural historian who has a particular interest in ecclesiastical buildings. He is consultant archaeologist to Salisbury Cathedral.